THE FUTURE OF CULTURAL MINORITIES

Also by the editors

Antony E. Alcock
THE HISTORY OF THE SOUTH TYROL QUESTION
HISTORY OF THE INTERNATIONAL LABOUR ORGANISATION

Brian K. Taylor
THE WESTERN LACUSTRINE BANTU

John M. Welton (*co-editor with Jack Walton*)
RATIONAL CURRICULUM PLANNING

THE FUTURE OF CULTURAL MINORITIES

Edited by

Antony E. Alcock
Brian K. Taylor
John M. Welton

M

First published 1979 by
THE MACMILLAN PRESS LTD
London and Basingstoke
Associated companies in Delhi
Dublin Hong Kong Johannesburg Lagos
Melbourne New York Singapore Tokyo

Typeset in Great Britain by
VANTAGE PHOTOTYPESETTING CO. LTD
SOUTHAMPTON AND LONDON
and printed by
UNWIN BROTHERS LIMITED
The Gresham Press,
Old Woking, Surrey.

British Library Cataloguing in Publication Data

The future of cultural minorities
1. Minorities
I. Alcock, Anthony Evelyn II. Taylor, Brian K
III. Welton, John
301.45'1 HT1523

ISBN 0-333-25597-6

Contents

Acknowledgements

In May 1977 the editors held a weekend seminar on 'The Future of Cultural Minorities' at the Richardson Institute for Peace and Conflict Research. Following the seminar the general form of this book emerged and the editors would like to record their gratitude to the Director of the Institute, Michael Nicholson, and to the Joseph Rowntree Charitable Trust for making the seminar possible. They also wish to thank the following people who contributed to the seminar: Ken Gladdish, Lars Mosesson, Claire Palley, Joseph Pickvance, Frances Pinter, Robert Ramsay, and Andrew Trew.

Several colleagues at the New University of Ulster contributed to our thinking about this book, among them Derek Birrell.

We thank all the contributors to this book for their interest, cooperation, and willingness to keep almost impossible deadlines.

Finally we would like to thank Nicholas Gillett whose gift it is to sow seeds.

Notes on the Contributors

Antony E. Alcock is Senior Lecturer and Head of West European Studies at the New University of Ulster, Coleraine. He previously held positions with the International Labour Organisation, the United Nations Institute for Training and Research, the European Commission and the European Economic and Social Council. He has written extensively on minority protection.

Ken Gladdish is Senior Lecturer in Politics at the University of Reading. He was formerly an Administrative Officer in Uganda. He has particular interests in multicultural problems.

Terence A. O'Brien is Lecturer in Economics at the New University of Ulster, Coleraine. He is engaged in a study of the role of co-operatives in the economic and social development of contemporary Ireland.

Claire Palley is Professor of Law at the University of Kent, Canterbury, and is particularly interested in constitutional and family law.

Glanville Price is Professor of Romance Languages at the University College of Wales, Aberystwyth. His particular interest lies in minority languages, and he has published *The Present Position of Minority Languages in Western Europe: a Selective Bibliography.*

Frederick Y. St Leger is Lecturer in Social Administration at the New University of Ulster, Coleraine. His recent research covers the African press in South Africa.

Margaret B. Sutherland is Professor of Education at the University of Leeds. She has special interests in comparative education.

Brian K. Taylor is Senior Lecturer in Social Administration at the New University of Ulster, Coleraine, and has previously held university posts at Swansea and Adelaide. He was formerly a social anthropologist and Community Development Officer in East Africa. He is editor of *Community Development Journal.*

John M. Welton is Lecturer in Educational Development and Administration at the New University of Ulster, Coleraine, and his research interests lie in the relationships between schools and the community.

Introduction

The idea of producing a work on the future of cultural minorities in the multicultural state had its origins in the discussion following the presentation of a paper by one of the editors at a Social Sciences Staff Research seminar at the New University of Ulster on the effect that the principle of equality of human rights was having on the position of cultural minorities.[1]

The political scientists, sociologists, historians and economists present brought different, and at times conflicting, perspectives to the problem, differences which are reflected in the literature on majority–minority relations. There are plenty of case studies of individual cultural minorities in relation to their host-state and, in many cases, in relation to other minorities in the host-state. There are studies of the practice of international organisation in regard to the problem of protecting minorities. However, there appears to be no work which sought to combine a variety of academic approaches to explore those factors which are or have been a source of concern or conflict in majority-minority as well as inter-minority relations. The aim of this book, therefore, is to contribute to the development of a general theory on the future of cultural minorities.

The editors were aware of the academic, political and ideological pitfalls which confronted them, each starting from a different academic and political position. One, a historian and political scientist, whose work in the field has tended to be minority-oriented, has noted the growing dissatisfaction with nation-states and the centralism and uniformism of so much of modern government that is leading to a revolt of the peripheral regions where so many minorities live. He is concerned at those trends in government that appear to rely too heavily on numbers and to pay too little heed to those who do not carry the big guns in society in the establishment of priorities, besides emphasising political and legal solutions to problems at the expense of economic, social and cultural factors and implications. The second, a social scientist, whose interests lie in the analysis of social and cultural change, considers the question of minority cultures in relation to what he sees as the on-going development of national and global societies and an associated convergence of cultures. To what extent can cultural minorities adapt themselves to, or resist, this trend? What are the factors which are likely to help or hinder them? What can they realistically hope to preserve or develop which is distinctively their own in the widening societies and less restrictive cultures of the future? The interests of the third, a sociologist and educationalist, lie in the need to know much more about the nature of forms of conflict which concern nearly every state in the world today.

These three areas of interest are, of course, complementary, but their latent disparity did mean that the problem of agreeing upon what they meant by the terms 'culture' and 'minority' had to be faced by the editors.

There was no difficulty in accepting that the definition of Sir Edward Tylor, that culture was 'that complex whole which includes knowledge, belief, art, morals, law, custom, and other capabilities and habits acquired by man as a member of society'[2] was most appropriate, particularly when considered together with that of Bronislaw Malinowski, that it was an 'instrumental apparatus by which man is put in a position the better to cope with the concrete specific problems that face him in his environment in the course of the satisfaction of his needs'.[3]

Some problems occurred, however, with finding an acceptable definition of the term 'minority'. Two definitions at present enjoy a wide circulation. Louis Wirth, writing in 1945, defined a minority as any group, racial or ethnic (cultural), the members of which, because of their physical or cultural characteristics, are singled out for differential and unequal treatment, and/or who regard themselves as objects of collective discrimination. For Wirth, a minority was essentially politically subordinate and, at the same time, often socially and economically disprivileged, socially isolated, spatially segregated and disaffected in its attitudes to its status.[4] It is interesting to note that while his definition embraced both racial and cultural minorities, his main concern was with the latter.

The definition elaborated by the United Nations in 1950 was more sharply focused on cultural minorities.[5] It similarly referred to both political and sociological factors. Minorities, in this view, were only those non-dominant groups in a population which, while being loyal to the nation-state, wished to preserve stable ethnic, religious or linguistic traditions markedly different from those of the rest of the population, and, moreover, were sufficiently large in numbers to be able to develop such characteristics spontaneously. The political phrase 'non-dominant' was used at the time to exclude from the need for protection those white populations that were in the ascendancy in Africa and Asia. Likewise, the reference to the need to be loyal in order to qualify for protection was motivated by the experience of German minorities in Poland and Czechoslovakia whose behaviour—in a relatively privileged position—was held to have undermined the nation of which they were part and contributed to the outbreak of the Second World War.

These definitions, however, were not entirely satisfactory.

Firstly, as phrased, they did not clarify whether or not they included other categories of 'group', such as women, the blind or homosexuals, who might be held to have, and wish to promote, a distinctive sub-culture. The editors felt that as these sets of people were not sub-societies in the sense of interconnected collectivities of families capable of sustaining a substantial cross-generational and cross-sexual culture they should be excluded from the definition.

Secondly, the United Nations reference to the preservation of traditions did not sufficiently clarify the degree of preservation desired. For example, many immigrant communities, such as the Italians in the United States and Indians in the United Kingdom maintain strong links with their traditional culture. Was the maintenance of such links sufficient to qualify these communities for inclusion as cultural minorities, and were they cultural minorities in the same sense as the French in Canada and the Dutch in South Africa? The editors felt that the qualification should be the public institutionalisation or the demand for public institutionalisation of the culture concerned. Thus it would be necessary to draw a distinction between those cultural groups whose efforts to retain links with their cultural past are limited to the private sphere of daily life, talking the language at home, in private commerce, at worship, or in social clubs, and who do not demand that the culture form part of national or regional educational systems, and those groups whose culture and language are officially recognised and who enjoy extensive facilities for their preservation and development, such as the French Canadians, or those who are actively seeking to propagate and institutionalise their culture, such as the Bretons, Spanish Basques and Catalans.

Thirdly, the term 'minority' in both the Wirth and United Nations definitions carried with it the implication that the groups in question are subject to adverse discrimination and domination by others, whereas this is not so in every case. Some, like the Afrikaners, are clearly dominant in the state; some, like the French Canadians and Aland Islanders, are dominant in a particular area of the state of which they are nationals, particularly if that area happens to be their historic homeland; and others may even be the object of very necessary discrimination in their favour. For these reasons it was decided to exclude any reference to domination in the editors' definition.

Fourthly, there was, at least in the Wirth definition, a lack of concern with the size of the minority. As all cultural minorities in the world appear to be numerical minorities in their nation-state, the editors felt that this attribute should be retained in their definition.

Fifthly, the United Nations definition implied that the minorities in question are rigid and monolithic in their linguistic and cultural traditions, yet, as the case of the various Celtic peoples show, there are important exceptions. For example, less than 30 per cent of Bretons, Scots, Irish, and Welsh speak their imputed native tongue.

The minorities with which this book is concerned, therefore, are cultural minorities, i.e., collectivities of families who previously constituted the whole or part of other nations or political societies in which they, or their ancestors, developed a distinctive culture, who have since been incorporated forcibly as by and through conquest, or voluntarily as by immigration, within a multicultural national society, and who now as numerical minorities in such societies preserve or wish to preserve part of their traditional or otherwise distinctive culture. It is concerned with what may be termed their current cultural status *vis-à-vis* that of other collectivities, whether the majority or other minorities, within the nation, and also with their cultural viability and cultural future. What scope is there for the preservation and/or development of distinctive minority cultures in the multicultural state?

The number and diversity of cultural minorities across the world will emerge in the chapters which follow, but the following examples may be helpful here. They include, in the Americas, the American Indian tribes of Peru, Mexico and the United States, and the French Canadians; in Europe, the South Tyrolese in Italy, the Swedes in Finland, Catalans and Basques in Spain, the Bretons in France, and the Catholics in Northern Ireland; in the Middle East, the Arabs in Israel, the Turks in Cyprus, and the Kurds in Iraq; in Africa, the Zulus and Afrikaners of South Africa, and the Ganda and Karamajong of Uganda; in Asia, the Tamils of Sri Lanka and the Shans and Arakanese of Burma; and in Oceania the Maoris of New Zealand and the Fijians of Fiji.

These minorities will be found to be diverse in their origin—some are indigenous, others are immigrant; they will be diverse in size relative to the national population—some are over 30 per cent, others are under 1 per cent; some will have kin-states, others will not; some will be politically dominant, others will be politically subordinate; some will be very dissatisfied with their present status and the prospects for their future, others will be relatively content; some will have cultures relatively similar to other cultures in the nation state, others will have very different cultures. It will be one of the objectives of the editors to explore the significance of these and the many other factors involved.

The promotion of a theory of cultural minorities will depend on analysis of culture on the one hand, and of society, the bearer of culture, on the other. This will facilitate the identification and characterisation of:

1. present-day minority cultures—what these constitute, how they relate to other cultures in the nation, and what distinctive and traditional aspects of them minorities are anxious to preserve and develop;

2. the forces playing upon them—the relative strength of economic, political, legal, religious, educational, mass-media and familial forces;

3. the changes taking place in them—whether and in what way they are being modified by the above-mentioned forces, and what traditional or distinctive parts, if any, are being preserved; and

4. feasible measures which might be taken to preserve them.

Two of the editors, partly as a result of their different backgrounds in Europe and Africa respectively, and partly as a result of their different political persuasion, began this enterprise with radically different interpretations of and attitudes to change in minority cultures. One visualised a minority culture as a relatively fixed entity shared by all members of the minority, distinctively different from the culture of other people in the state, and something which in general the minority wished to preserve as a distinctive totality. It was being subjected first to the destructive forces of a remote, bureaucratic, alien central government with a passion for majority rule, 'equality' and social uniformity, and secondly, to the corrosive effects of natural economic and social developments. All this was resulting in the erosion of the minority culture. The minority was greatly concerned with this threat to its identity; it wished to remain different as it had always been; and special measures for its cultural preservation were therefore a necessity.

The other conceived of a minority culture as a more dynamic differentiated entity, not all of which was necessarily exclusive to minority members, not all of which was different from the culture of others in the society, and not all of which all the minority necessarily wanted to preserve. It was being subjected to many forces, both constructive and destructive. This was resulting in the modernisation and development of some parts of the traditional culture, the replacement of some parts and the preservation of others. In relatively free and open societies, this was probably, on the whole, a healthy adaptation to a constantly changing situation. The minority was by no means opposed to all the changes concerned. Some might like to see more change. There might be an argument for special protective measures in some cases but generally, at least in democratic societies, minorities could probably take steps themselves to preserve what was both distinctive and of lasting value in their culture. Should not the aim be to work for both unity and diversity in the modern multicultural state, but should not scarce resources be devoted rather to the promotion of the former than to any artificial preservation of the latter?

It is hoped that these different orientations will not bias but will rather stimulate the analysis which follows. Forewarned readers, however, have been forearmed.

The mode of presentation of the book will be as follows.

Chapter 1 considers the light which that branch of social theory known as cultural theory can throw on the future of cultural minorities in the multicultural state. Chapters 2 to 5 analyse the linguistic, educational, mass-media and economic dimensions. Chapter 6 examines the development of governmental attitudes to minorities in western industrial states. Chapter 7 considers constitutional arrangements for the preservation and development of minority cultures, and Chapter 8 discusses the political dynamics of minority–majority relationships. The final Chapter sets out conclusions and provides pointers for the development of a theory of cultural minorities.

NOTES

1. A. E. Alcock, 'A New Look at Protection of Minorities and the Principle of Equality of Human Rights' in *Community Development Journal* vol. 12, no. 2 (Oxford, 1977), pp. 85–95.
2. Sir E. Tylor, *Primitive Culture* (London, 1871).
3. B. Malinowski, *A Scientific Theory of Culture* (Chapel Hill, 1944), p. 36.
4. L. Wirth, 'The Problem of Minority Groups' in R. Linton (ed.), *The Science of Man in the World Crisis* (New York, 1945).
5. T. H. Bagley, *General Principles and Problems in the International Protection of Minorities* (Geneva, 1950), pp. 178 ff.

1 Culture: Whence, Whither and Why?

Brian K. Taylor

What light can that branch of social theory known as cultural theory throw on the future of cultural minorities in the multicultural state? One would expect that a crucial contribution would be to our understanding of the nature, origins and development of culture in general, and the culture of minority groups in particular.

THE NATURE OF CULTURE

Human cultures were early conceived to be the total, standardised and established way of life (customs and institutions) and the total way of thought (knowledge, beliefs and values) of particular peoples or societies, considered as wholes. Tylor's famous and much-quoted 1871 definition of culture is a typical and still useful anthropological example: 'That complex whole which includes knowledge, belief, art, morals, law, custom and other capabilities and habits acquired by man as a member of society.'[1] Others have illustrated its even greater complexity by reference to additional components like language, literature, philosophy, religion, science and technology.

This sum total of interconnected cultural components can be divided into *social organisation* (the way a particular people organise themselves into groups of distinctive kinds, and the way they organise their activities in customs, institutions, etc), *technology* (the artifacts and techniques of material culture), and *ideological systems* (their systems of knowledge, beliefs, values and expressive symbols).

This is not the place for a history of cultural definitions which have been legion,[2] but it should be noted that there is still considerable variation in usage, some sociologists for example preferring to exclude social organisation and technology, and to confine the term to ideological components. The comprehensive conception including all three types of dimension, being more relevant to our purposes, will be employed in this chapter.

In seeking explanations of culture in this sense one is seeking to explain not all of a people's activities, ideas and material instruments but rather those which have become organised, systematised and standardised, and which are incorporated in the ongoing life and thought of the people or otherwise maintained, for example in stores or records, for possible future use. All this remains a very complex whole and, some would say, an analytically unmanageable whole which needs to be broken down into sub-cultural components which are carefully related to society's group components before any very convincing explanations can become possible.

Nevertheless, explanations of the total culture of a people have been attempted and it will be useful to make brief reference to these first. Culture, that is the social organisation, technology and ideological systems (or as Sorokin called them the behavioural, material and ideological cultures)[3] which are maintained by a people, is now generally accepted to be a natural rather than a supernatural product, and more precisely a social rather than a genetic natural product, a contemporary and historical precipitate of the life and experience of men both living and dead. It is a social heritage but more than a heritage; it is, as Raymond Firth described it, 'the active component of accumulated resources, immaterial as well as material, which the people inherit, employ, transmute, add to and transmit'.[4]

Before considering how this social product, with its historical and contemporary components, has been explained it may be useful to illustrate, very briefly, how total cultures have been classified. In the organisational dimension, cultures have been distinguished in general terms related, for example, to types of economic organisation like hunting, fishing and gathering; pastoralism; agriculture; and industry;[5] to types of political organisation like primitive stateless societies; primitive states; city states and empires; feudal states; and nation-states and empires;[6] and to types of religious organisation like family cults; kinship religions and cults; local religions and cults; tribal or folk religions and cults; national or state religions and cults; and universal religions and cults.[7] Similar classifications can be produced in the domestic, linguistic, economic control, administrative, political control and other fields.

In the technological dimension, cultures have been distinguished in general categories like hunting and gathering technology (characterised by wooden, stone and bone tools and weapons; firemaking; and a human energy base); subsistence agricultural and/or pastoral technology (metal tools and weapons; and a human and animal energy base); commercial agricultural and craft technology (metal tools and weapons; animal-driven ploughs and wheeled vehicles; sailing ships; writing; money; gunpowder; cannon; hand guns; and an additional energy base of water and wind); and industrial technology (machines, steam ploughs, motor tractors, machine guns, steam locomotives, steamships, motor vehicles, aircraft, spacecraft; telegraph, record-player, telephone, radio, cinema, television, computers, etc; with an additional steam, petrol, electricity, solar and nuclear-energy base).[8]

Lastly, in the ideological dimension cultures have been classified in general terms like theological, metaphysical and scientific or positive;[9] or analytical (scientific), synthetic (religious and philosophical), symbolic (artistic) and practical (technological);[10] or ideational, idealistic and materialistic or sensate;[11] or mythopoeic-and-religious, and speculative-and-scientific.[12]

THE EXPLANATION OF CULTURE AND CULTURES

Explanations of why all peoples and societies, be they prehistorical, historical or contemporary, have had total cultures, each with some universal characteristics like organisation, technology and ideology, have been couched in very general, and sometimes platitudinous terms. This culture has been conceived as a response to human needs, and as a vast, 'instrumental apparatus by which man is put in a position the better to cope with the concrete specific problems that face him in his environment in the course of the satisfaction of his needs'.[13] It is an instrumental, interpretative and expressive means of adapting to, and coming to terms with, man's physical, biological, social and cultural environment. It is a mechanism which serves men's needs both spiritual and material.[14] It is a means of utilising the resources of the environment in the service of man.[15]

The general rather than particular similarities of human cultures—their universal elements or dimensions—have commonly been attributed on the one hand to the 'general likeness in human nature' or mankind and on the other to the 'general likeness in the circumstances of life' or the human environment.[16] Broadly similar humans through the ages and across the earth have responded in broadly similar ways to broadly similar challenges. For this reason all peoples have had families, marriage, tools, property, religion, art, etc. of some type.

Broad explanations of this kind are often phrased in a way that suggests that a culture is acquired[17] and shared[18] and transmitted[19] by all members of a society, and that it is equally functional or beneficial for them all. This erroneous interpretation seems partly to have been the consequence of failing to identify those who 'establish or invent', 'maintain', 'transmit', 'acquire', 'utilise', 'modify', 'do not utilise', and 'dispense with' different components of the total-culture, and thus failing to recognise significant differences in the resources, power, interests, cultural roles and cultural influences of different groups within society.

Culture, to be sure, is the sum total of all the active and maintained apparatus of a society but it is arguable that the creation or establishment, the maintenance or organisation, the transmission, and the development or improvement of much of it has been due to the efforts of a relatively small number of individuals and groups in that society. This suggestion may be productively pursued when we pass, as we do now, to the more interesting and challenging questions of why there are particular similarities and differences in human cultures, why cultures change, and what the major trends in cultural change in our time seem to be. Attention will be confined to socio-cultural explanations and predictions.

If two or more societies have similar cultures or cultural systems this is usually attributed either to their having acquired or adopted them from the same or similar external or foreign sources[20] (the culture in effect having been 'diffused' by migration, colonisation, missionary activity, conquest, commerce, education or other influence in foreign lands, mass communications, influence of resident foreigners, etc.) or to their having independently and spontaneously established or invented them, or developed them along parallel or converging lines with the same general result[21] (the culture in effect having been 'evolved' to the same level), or again to a combination of such diffusion and evolution.

Some anthropologists consider that most cultures while influenced by both processes owe the bulk of their content to diffusion rather than to independent development or evolution.[22] Others have indicated, at least with reference to less modifiable organisational aspects of culture, that certain cultural similarities, e.g. in the form of family, marriage, kin and clan groups, rules of residence and descent, and types of kinship terminology were found in many, previously unconnected, parts of the world and cannot be explained in terms of diffusion.[23] The pyramids of widely separated Egypt and Mexico have been interpreted in the same way.

In similar fashion different cultures or cultural systems have been 'explained' in terms of different diffusionary sources like, for example, British, Dutch and French colonial powers, or in terms of independent and spontaneous inventions or innovations, and evolutionary development of these components of organisation, technology and ideology by different peoples, possibly with different resources and in response to different situations, along differing or diverging lines.

THE EXPLANATION OF CULTURAL CHANGE

Archaeological, historical and ethnographic evidence has revealed not only the differences and resemblances of cultures but also how cultures have changed over time. It is now generally accepted that cultures have changed, or, more precisely, peoples have changed their cultures, gradually or by revolutions, as sequential adaptations to continuing or changing situations. Both the 'line' of adaptive sequence and the stages, whether of development or regression, through which cultures have been changed have varied in different societies. Thus with regard to cultural systems of an economic kind some have been changed in a capitalist and others in a socialist line or direction, and again some have been developed to the industrial 'stage' through intervening stages different from those of other industrialised societies. At the same time, notwithstanding this multilinear and multistage form of cultural change, some analysts claim that mankind as a whole has in the long run been changing its cultures in what is proving to be a single progressive and developing direction, and that these cultures despite oscillations and setbacks have been developed through broadly similar general stages. We shall return to this subject in the section on current trends in cultural change.

In considering the *why* of cultural change it is vital to resist the tendency which has long bedevilled social and cultural analysis, to reify culture, and to speak, for example, as if it has a life of its own, diffusing here and evolving or developing there, quite apart from the individuals and groups who create, conserve, enforce, transmit, adopt and modify it. Connected with this, and equally obstructive, has been the tendency, which is still apparent, to explain cultural and cultural change in terms of other disembodied cultural abstractions like 'ideas' and 'technology' which are often treated as if they are autonomous active agents or efficient causes.[24]

As it is men who have created culture and cultural systems, and men who seek to conserve or change them, both cultural order and cultural change must largely be explained in social structural terms, that is, in terms of the individuals and groups of society, and the interactive relationships between them. It is in this co-operating, competing and conflicting social context that reference to 'ideas', 'technology' and so on becomes appropriate and may prove fruitful in sociocultural analysis.

A further necessity in cultural explanation is to recognise not only that cultures or cultural systems are group-based, but that in each case their different elements—the organisational, technological and ideological elements which were separated above for ease of analysis—are in reality interconnected. In other words, one must be careful to identify the group or groups who established, maintained, modified or contributed to the disappearance of a cultural system which included an organisation, a technology and an ideology, all together constituting an apparatus thought to be worth preserving, modifying or discarding as the case might be.

To understand the creation, continuity and change of culture one must also pay close attention to the group *forces* or pressures involved, and particularly to the resources or assets the control of which gives the groups what power they possess. As the resources or assets are usually unequally distributed in society some groups will obviously have more effect on cultural creation, continuity or change than others. The social situation, of course, is always a dynamic one so if there are to be realistic predictions of cultural change study must be made of changes in society's power-base resulting from on-going changes in resources and resource control.

In large, differentiated and stratified societies in particular many groups will have a bearing on culture, and these will need to be visualised as components of interactive systems within society, standing in some postulated relationship to one another within the systems, and within society as a whole. As yet the social sciences do not appear to have made much progress in the development of such social structural models.

Thus in complex modern societies different categories of group—governmental, political, mass-media, economic, religious, health, educational, welfare, recreational, family and others—can easily be identified. Each has its own group culture and each has some potential for influencing the culture of others. It has proved more difficult, however, to establish how these various groups are interconnected in different, sometimes overlapping interactive systems, and just how they affect one another.

Which of these groups determine the culture of a people? Which of these groups have most influence on cultural systems, that is the institutionalised ways of life: the type of groups people maintain, and the way they organise activities in them; the things they own and produce, and the technology they employ; and their established ways of thought and expression? In other words, which of these groups have most influence on the continuity or the change of this vast cultural apparatus?

Cultural analysis will probably be facilitated by first identifying, at the risk of over-simplification, those groups within a society—the *conservative groups*—who maintain or transmit culture, and the way in which they exercise this cultural control, e.g. in the case of cultural maintenance, by the enforcement of laws, rules, regulations and procedures (whether of legal, religious, moral, occupational or other kinds), or in the case of cultural transmission, by bequest of property, or by education, training, propaganda and mass-communication. To some extent, of course, all established groups are conservative but what seems to be worth ascertaining are those groups who have most culture (laws, procedures; property; ideas and values) to maintain, and most to transmit, and who by reason of control of considerable human and economic resources, i.e. staff and property, have the power and capacity to do this. Having identified such groups—they may for example be governmental, political, economic, religious, mass-media, educational and familial—it might prove easier to establish whether some of these 'conservative' groups—of different types e.g. economic and political or of the same type e.g. economic—work together, in competition or in conflict in what is, in effect, the business of maintaining or transmitting culture.

Secondly, one can identify those groups—the *reformist* groups—who in pursuit of their interests have become dissatisfied with some aspect of the established culture and are seeking to change or replace or make significant additions to it. While all groups may be reformist in the sense that they find it necessary at some time to modify their culture the notion is here used for groups who are pressing for more radical changes, for example for the establishment of radically new forms of group or procedure or technology or product or ideology or form of expression. Into this category would come some political parties and pressure groups, professional associations, trade unions, consumer associations, student groups, citizen groups, etc. The outcome of their reformist endeavours will depend on the power they exert *vis-à-vis* that of more conservative groups, and as this depends on the resources or assets they have managed to mobilise and organise for reform these too need to be investigated.

Thirdly, one can distinguish those groups (or more precisely those classes or publics)—the *adoptive* classes—who adopt or accept culture and make it their own. These might equally be called *conforming* classes if conformity did not often connote a passive, unthinking, almost automatic reaction whereas much culture is acquired and pursued in a more conscious and active way. The adoptive classes—who form the bulk of any societal population—are those who utilise the cultural apparatus which some of the established groups maintain or transmit. They are the people who join or use or otherwise accept the established groups of society, who practise the institutionalised ways of life, who use the standardised products and technology, and who subscribe to the received ideas, values and beliefs. They are, for example, either the ordinary membership—as distinguished from the controllers and organisers—of established groups, or, as non-members, the users, readers, listeners, viewers, consumers, clients or adherents of the cultural products of those groups.

Fourthly, and finally, it may be useful in cultural analysis to identify those groups—the *creative* groups—who devise, invent, originate, evolve or develop new forms of organisational, technological or ideological culture. These are the individuals and groups who produced the culture which is now maintained, transmitted or modified by established groups both conservative and radical, and which is adopted and practised by the classes who are 'members' of those groups or outside 'consumers' of their cultural 'products'. Much of any contemporary culture will of course have been 'created' or produced by individuals and groups long dead, many of them now hidden in the mists of time. One would therefore be concerned here to identify contemporary creative groups, and once again the controlled resources or assets on which their power depends. Examples of such groups are planning groups, scientific research and development groups, creative arts groups, and scientific, artistic, religious, philosophical and professional societies and associations. Some of these may be based in government or business sectors, others may enjoy greater autonomy, e.g. in universities and research institutes, but most are likely to be highly dependent on financial aid from other groups.

CURRENT TRENDS IN CULTURAL CHANGE

Several broad trends of cultural change within societies across the world can be suggested. These can be conveniently covered by reference to the three categories, social organisation, technology and ideology previously employed. It is not implied that these trends are equally apparent in all countries but rather that there are widespread indications of them in all world regions. The interconnections between organisation, technology and ideology should be borne in mind.

In the organisational dimension on-going *economic trends* include the increasing use of specialised economic groups in more commercialised, industrialised, social-service economies, the employment of a science-based technology, the concentration of economic power in large-scale, urbanised enterprises (whether private or public) employing increasingly skilled workforces, the extension of economic group influence within city-based regions and further afield in the nation and sometimes across the world, and the increased control of economic activities by governments.

Associated with these developments, and having an important bearing on cultural continuity and change, has been the emergence of new *economic classes*, that is sets of people standing in the same interactive position relative to one another in economic systems whether in individual firms or industries or in the national economy as a whole. Thus, for example, in each, say, mining firm or organisation and in its sphere of influence there are different classes like—and here we necessarily simplify the situation—a controlling class, a subordinate working class, a consuming class, and others. Again, in the mining industry as a whole one can identify a mining industry controlling class, working class, consuming class and so on, these being composed of the separate mining organisational classes previously mentioned. And similarly, in the economy as a whole, that is in all the industries taken together, that is agricultural, mining, manufacturing, etc. it is useful to recognise that controlling, working, consuming, etc. classes have emerged, or are emerging.

These economic classes, whether viewed in the firm, industrial or national economic sense, and whether at local, regional or national levels, have different interests, by reason of their situation, and different capacities for preserving or changing the economic culture. It is possible that they have, or will develop, different economic ideologies, e.g. ideals about the future control of economic affairs. What type of control will emerge will largely depend on the disposition and deployment of the forces available to the parties concerned. Part of this force will surely depend on how the different classes organise themselves and their resources, and what power they can muster and apply. The on-going emergence and development of workers' and consumers' organisations may suggest a growing, if long-term, drive for economic control and development along more public lines. The earlier classification of cultural groups and classes into conservative, reformist, adoptive and creative can be applied to economic groups and classes, and may have some analytical value here.

Turning to *political trends* it is possible to identify the increasing use of specialised political, governmental and administrative groups involved in more democratic, technocratic and bureaucratic activities, the employment once again of an increasingly scientific technology, the concentration of political power in large-scale organisations like parties, unions and departments, employing increasingly skilled workforces, and the extension of political and governmental influence over all spheres of life across the nation.

Associated with these developments, and having a bearing on cultural continuity and change, has been the emergence of new *political classes* in the separate political or governmental organisations and their spheres of influence, in the different political sectors, and in the polity as a whole. Once again one can identify political controlling, working and consumer (or client) classes which for cultural analysis can be related to the cultural groups and classes previously described.

Trends in religious organisation on present evidence are more difficult to identify but there are surely indications of the increasing differentiation of churches and sects, more emphasis on universalist rather than tribal or national beliefs, more democratic participation by laymen in church affairs, less rigid insistence on traditional beliefs and rituals, and a decreasing influence of religious organisations on the economy, on government and on education. As in other spheres so in the religious sphere, groups and classes can be identified, and thereafter be reinterpreted as cultural groups and cultural classes.

Finally, in the examples being suggested here, there are important *educational and mass-communication trends*. These include the increasing use of specialised educational groups like schools, technical colleges and universities; and mass-media groups like newspaper, cinema, radio, record and television companies or corporations, both types of group contributing to the spread of universal and national rather than purely local, and modern rather than traditional, pictures of the world, the employment of a science-based technology and an increasingly skilled and professionalised workforce, the concentration of educational and communication power in large-scale organisations or systems, the extension of their influence throughout the nation, and sometimes further afield, and the increased control of educational and mass-media activities by governments, and in the case of the media by powerful business corporations as well. The reinterpretation of the groups and classes within educational and mass-media systems as cultural groups and classes, whether conservative, reformist, adoptive or creative, would appear to be particularly relevant.

Our treatment of organisational trends makes a separate outline of technological and ideological trends unnecessary. We have already suggested with regard to the first that the world-wide trend is towards a science-based technology. In the second, namely ideological dimension of ideas and values, significant trends can be identified with regard to the two classes of ideas—*existential* empirical or non-empirical ideas, and *normative* ideas—proposed by Talcott Parsons.[25] These trends seem to be towards more scientific and secular thought in the first case and more democratic and secular values in the second. This steadily changing orientation will probably have important implications, in the long run, for more technocratic and democratic control of governments and economies.

THE ANALYSIS OF SUB-CULTURES

So far, we have focused on the nature and development of total cultures, that is the overall cultures of 'peoples' or national societies, and how, across the world, due to a combination of exogenous (diffused) and endogenous (independently developed or evolved) factors, there seem to be signs of a broad cultural convergence. Attention, however, has also been directed to the underlying group-basis of the national culture, and the varying involvement of different groups and classes within it.

We pass now to the analysis of national *sub-cultures* dealing firstly with sub-cultures within a broadly homogeneous national culture, and secondly with sub-cultures within the more heterogeneous culture of a multicultural state, i.e. a state containing cultural minorities. Can it be that there are signs of convergence at the sub-cultural level also, and if so, in what sense, if at all, are cultural minorities likely to 'survive'?

Even in a small, structurally simple and culturally 'homogeneous' society sets of people, or more precisely sets of families, can be identified who, while sharing part of the total-societal-culture have, in other respects, a distinctive way of life. When such 'homogeneous' national societies grow in size and structural complexity, that is with increasing territorial spread and increasing social differentiation and stratification there may be further variation in such 'ways of life'. It is useful to refer to the overall culture of these sets of people as a 'sub-culture'.

The term 'sub-culture' can, and has been used, for the cultural patterns of any category of individual persons like 'women', 'youth' and 'delinquents'. It has been used for the cultural patterns of any group or type of group within the national society like the sub-culture of the family, school, gang,[26] hospital, prison, factory, political-party, department or church. Another usage, which we employ here, is to confine the term to the cultural patterns of larger sets of people—collectivities,[27] sub-societies,[28] regional or other communities, etc.—who include 'both sexes, all ages and family groups'[29] and who, by reason of their use during the life cycle of the same type of network of groups and institutions, have come generally to share the same situation in life.

For ease of reference we shall call such sets of people 'sub-societies' and their total culture their 'sub-culture'. It is important to recognise that not all of a sub-culture will be distinctive or 'separate characteristics' of the sub-society.[30] Some of it will constitute 'national' cultural elements shared by all other sub-societies; some may be 'sub-national' elements found also in at least one of the other sub-societies; and some will be elements distinctive to the sub-society concerned.

Within a large 'homogeneous' society, i.e. one without minorities, increases in the numbers and spread of population, together with urban concentration, have often led to the establishment of regional and local communities (sub-societies) with regional and local *community sub-cultures.* Within each such community or sub-society differentiation may have given rise to *religious* sub-societies with *religious sub-cultures,* some of which may be common to sets of people in other communities in part of or across the entire nation. Again, within the communities, and across the nation, economic concentration and stratification may have contributed to the development of classes with *class sub-cultures.* These classes can be visualised as strata cutting horizontally across the 'vertical' once-for-all division of regions and local communities, and across the vertical, sometimes duplicated divisions of religious sub-societies.

Employing some such dimensions it is obviously possible to identify sets of people—where the class strata intersect the religious and community divisions—who have a broadly similar sub-cultural 'core'. Examples would be middle-class Protestants in the rural mid-west or, say, Shropshire, and working-class Catholics in urban New England, or, say, Yorkshire. Other refinements in this classification, like gradations in the class divisions, are possible but in the present context need not be explored.

Reference was earlier made to the increased number and range of different groups spread across the modern nation who are involved in the creation, maintenance or enforcement, transmission or communication, and modification of culture, and how the bulk of the population with a measure, but only a measure, of free choice adopt or use the cultural procedures, products, ideas, values, etc. of some or other of these established—conservative or reformist, conflicting, competing or co-operating—groups. Examples of such influential cultural groups are business firms, professional associations, trade unions, political parties, government departments, mass-media corporations and churches. The emanating culture does not always derive from a centralised body: it may be transmitted from regional or local centres, but in either case the patterns are often uniform throughout the country. Thus the citizens of a modern state tend for the most part to experience, across the nation, the influence of the same types of food shop, book shop, record shop, factory, office, library, cinema, radio and television stations, newspaper companies, school, university, hospital, post office, welfare office, petrol station, police station, church and so on. From these and other such groups they derive many of the organisational, technological and ideological components of their culture.

These national or nationally distributed groups obviously contribute a large and growing 'national' component to the sub-culture of the sub-society. If our interpretation of cultural trends is broadly correct it would seem, with regard to sub-cultures in a 'homogeneous national culture', that sub-societies will become increasingly less exclusive and enclosed, and the content of their sub-cultures less distinctive to themselves. This convergence or standardisation of much of the sub-cultures is of course never complete. It may be closest at first among sets of people who are members of the same class.

How different is the position of minority sub-cultures in the more heterogeneous national culture of a 'multicultural state'? And what are the prospects of minorities preserving within their sub-cultures a large component peculiar and distinctive to themselves?

Cultural minorities are here taken to be collectivities of families previously constituting the whole or part of other nations or political societies in which they, or their ancestors, developed a distinctive culture, who have since been incorporated, forcibly as by and through conquest or enslavement, or voluntarily as through union or immigration, within a national society where they are now sub-societies with sub-cultures which still contain a large and traditional or otherwise distinctive component, and with populations which are usually less than half that of the nation as a whole.

Examples are the American Indians and the Negroes, together with the Irish, Italians and other immigrants in the United States, the French in Canada, the Welsh together with the Scots and the various immigrant groups in the United Kingdom, and the Zulus and other African, Asian and coloured peoples in South Africa. It should be noted that the definition employed does not imply that a minority's distinctive sub-culture always necessarily includes any particular component like a distinctive language or technology or religion. Nor does it imply that the minority wishes to preserve all of this traditional culture or that it adopts any particular attitude to its present and future collective status, or that it is necessarily discriminated against.[31]

Within a large society with a heterogeneous culture, that is a multicultural state with minorities, each minority population, unless it is concentrated in one region or local area, will come to be divided and constitute the whole or part of different communities. Associated with this location minority members will acquire a *community* component in their sub-culture. Within the community or communities the minority, unless it adheres completely to one religion, may be further divided and constitute the whole or part of different religious sub-societies. Associated with this affiliation minority members will acquire a *religious* component in their sub-culture. Again within the regional and local communities the minority, unless it is confined to one class, will come to be divided and constitute the whole or part of different classes. This class position will contribute a *class* component to the sub-culture.

The sub-culture of the minority, conceived as a whole, is that part of the national culture which is shared by the minority. Part of it will necessarily be 'national' elements shared with all other sub-societies in the nation. Part will constitute sub-national elements found also in one or more of the other sub-societies. And part will be the distinctive and separate characteristics of the minority. On what does the distinctive component of a minority sub-culture depend?

The degree of distinctiveness of a minority's sub-culture, and some of the factors which influence it, can initially be examined by reference to some of the dimensions of culture previously outlined. How much of its social organisation, for example, is distinctive to the minority? Does it have any special types of group like joint or extended families or clans or age-sets; or any special procedures or institutions whether domestic like recipes and meal customs, familial and kinship like endogamy, polygamy and patrilineal descent, linguistic like a language or dialect, artistic like music, songs, dances, painting, sculpture and literature, recreational like games, sports and amusements, economic like the Muslim prohibition of interest or the system of land ownership, political like hereditary leaders, and religious like church ritual and ceremonies?

Secondly, how much of its technology is distinctive to the minority? Does it have any special tools, weapons, utensils, instruments, vehicles and machines? Thirdly, how much of its ideology is distinctive? Does it have any special scientific, historical, religious, philosophical or artistic knowledge and beliefs? Does it have any special and different perspective on the world?

Similar questions can be asked with reference to the three types of sub-culture earlier described. How much of the minority's community, religious or class sub-culture is distinctive to itself?

Consideration of these questions in the case of the minority examples cited, viz. American Indians, Negroes and American Irish and Italians; the French in Canada; Welsh and Scots and, say, Pakistanis in Britain, and the Zulus and coloureds of South Africa will remind us that these peoples—at the time of their incorporation in their new national societies—entered the situation with cultural backgrounds variously different from the dominant or 'host' culture. This *original degree of cultural difference* is the first of the influencing factors to which we draw attention. This varying difference, indicated especially by major differences, and major combinations of differences, in social organisation like language, economy and government; in technology like money and machines; and in ideology like religion and level of scientific advancement, has surely been one of the determinants of the present degree of distinctiveness of a minority's sub-culture.[32]

At first sight this might suggest that the greater the original difference the greater the present distinctiveness but this would be to fail to take into account a second factor, viz. *the historical and current relative effectiveness of the different cultural components involved.* Minorities will surely seek to preserve only what they regard as the superior elements of their traditional culture? The relative quality of that culture and not just its degree of difference is clearly important.

It is not enough, however, for a minority to value some effective item of its traditional culture like its language or religion and to seek to preserve it. A third factor is *the capacity or power of the minority to maintain and transmit the distinctive culture.* This power will depend on, *inter alia*, the resources, e.g. leadership, population size, economic assets and population support possessed. It may also be supplemented by aid from a kin-state.

A fourth factor affecting the degree of distinctiveness of a minority's sub-culture is *the degree of sub-societal residential and organisational enclosure currently maintained*,[33] that is the extent to which the minority by choice or necessity reside in separate areas within the national territory like 'homelands', regions, reservations or neighbourhoods, and the extent to which, again by choice or necessity, they live a separate and exclusive social life (endo-conviviality and endogamy) and belong to or otherwise use separate and exclusive minority organisations like schools, hospitals, clubs, restaurants, cinemas, transport services, churches, business firms, professional or occupational associations, mass-media organisations, unions, political parties, government departments, and universities. Some extreme cases of such social differentiation along religious and 'racial' lines have been reported from the Netherlands[34] and South Africa[35] respectively.

In addition to the vertical differentiation factor is a fifth factor which relates to horizontal division, viz. *the degree of sub-societal class enclosure*, that is the extent to which the minority are concentrated in particular economic classes. A tentative example here is the concentration of many Africans in South Africa within the lower working class, a stratum lower than that of the white upper working class.

Finally, in the variables to be mentioned, there is a sixth factor, viz. *the degree of freedom permitted minority group members, as individuals, to maintain, modify or discard their traditional culture.* This relates to pressures brought to bear on these individuals both by minority and 'majority' groups and leaders. Thus family heads and religious heads in some minorities may adopt extremely rigid attitudes against change. Again, the governments of multicultural societies may favour rigid policies *for* change like the earlier Australian policy of assimilation for the Aborigines or *against* change like the segregation or *apartheid* policy in South Africa.

With factors such as those suggested in mind we can now return to consider the prospects of minorities preserving in their sub-cultures a large component peculiar and distinctive to themselves. What is the future of cultural minorities in the multicultural state?

It is surely likely, across the world, and in most modern or modernising nations that minorities in the next century will form part of increasingly wide-span, differentiated and stratified, scientific and secular national societies in which a higher proportion of individual citizens, minority citizens included, will seek the best possible education; wish to move freely to, and advance in, the best possible places of work, residence and recreation, and choose freely from the best possible range of mass-media and other social services, technological equipment, and scientific, religious, philosophical and artistic systems of thought and expression; and come to expect that all institutions, whether traditional or modern, should be subjected to more rational scrutiny and more popular or democratic control?

Be that as it may, there is already evidence that minority sub-societies themselves have become firstly more differentiated, e.g., spread out in different regions and neighbourhoods and divided in different industries and occupational groups, different pressure groups and political parties, different social and recreational clubs and associations, and different churches, and in their use of different newspapers and other mass-media services; and secondly, more stratified in different economic classes.

This reduction in the degree of sub-societal residential and organisational enclosure—our fourth factor above—and reduction in the degree of sub-societal class enclosure—our fifth factor—have undoubtedly reduced the degree of distinctiveness of the minority's sub-culture.

In the process of the minority's widening of its social life beyond the confines of the collectivity—and this would appear to have happened among indigenous minorities like the North American

Indians, the Welsh and the Zulus and among immigrant minorities like the American Irish—the national and supra-minority sub-national components of their sub-cultures have increased while their separate and distinctive components, including their homeland or regional components, have decreased.

Is there any reason why this type of cultural change should not continue in future? It does not represent the replacement of a fixed traditional culture with an equally fixed alien culture. It is rather an adaptation made by minorities and non-minorities alike to a changing situation in which the best possible cultural instruments, minority or non-minority, national or foreign, traditional or modern, or some combination of these, are employed.

This is to suggest not that minority sub-cultures will necessarily dwindle to the point of extinction but rather—at least in free and open societies and with regard to minorities without advanced kin states—that by the incorporation of superior external elements where considerable international or national convergence is possible the distinctive minority component will probably be reduced to an essential core. It may well prove that this core is largely the 'expressive' and interpretive core of what remains distinctive and valuable in language, literature and the arts, and in folk lore and history. This core of culture, like all culture, however important, remains the creation and instrument of man. There may be magic but there is nothing sacrosanct about it. Whether the minorities of a free and open society will preserve it in future will surely, in the end, depend on their estimate of its quality at that time.

NOTES

1. Sir E. Tylor, *Primitive Culture* (London, 1871), vol. 1, p. 1.
2. A. L. Kroeber and Clyde Kluckhohn, 'Culture; a Critical Review of Concepts and Definitions', *Ethnology*, vol. 47, no. 1 (1952).
3. P. A. Sorokin, *Society, Culture and Personality* (New York, Harper and Brothers, 1947), pp. 313–24.
4. R. Firth, *Elements of Social Organisation* (London, Watts, 1951), p. 27.
5. The classifications of A. Ferguson (1767), Adam Smith (1776), K. Marx (1857–58; 1859; 1893–4), Lewis H. Morgan (1877), G. Gordon Childe (1936; 1942; 1951), Leslie A. White (1949; 1954) and Julian H. Steward (1955) can be productively compared.
6. Compare the approach of H. S. Maine (1861), L. H. Morgan (1877), M. Fortes and E. E. Evans-Pritchard (1940), R. H. Lowie (1950), A. Southall (1953), I. Schapera (1956), M. G. Smith (1956) and D. Easton (1954).

7. Compare the approach of Fustel de Coulanges (1864), E. B. Tylor (1891), C. P. Thiele (1897–99), L. Levy-Bruhl (1910, 1922), E. Durkheim (1912), M. Weber (1922), R. H. Lowie (1925), P. Radin (1937), J. Wach (1944), R. N. Bellah (1964) and E. E. Evans-Pritchard (1965).
8. History of Technology entry by R. A. Buchanan in *Encyclopaedia Britannica* (15th ed. 1974), vol. 18, pp. 24–54.
   S. Lilley, *Men, Machines and History* (London, 1965).
   R. A. Buchanan, *Technology and Social Progress* (London: Pergamon Press, 1965).
9. A. Comte, *Positive Philosophy*, tr. Martineau (New York, 1853), vol. 1, Chapters 1, 2, vol. 11, Chapter 6; *The System of Positive Polity* (New York, 1854), vol. III, Chapter 1.
10. E. de Roberty (1904, 1918), cited in P. A. Sorokin, *op. cit.*, p. 667.
11. P. A. Sorokin, *op. cit.*, Chapter 17.
12. Compare H. Frankfort, *The Intellectual Adventure of Ancient Man* (Chicago, 1946), and E. Cassirer, *An Essay on Man: an Introduction to a Philosophy of Human Culture* (Yale, 1944).
13. B. Malinowski, *A Scientific Theory of Culture* (Chapel Hill, 1944), p. 36.
14. L. A. White, *The Evolution of Culture* (London, 1959), pp. 8–10.
15. Julian S. Huxley, 'Evolution, Cultural and Biological' in W. L. Thomas (ed.), *Current Anthropology* (1956).
16. E. B. Tylor, *op. cit.*, p. 6.
17. E. B. Tylor, *op. cit.*, p. 15.
18. Talcott Parsons, *The Social System* (Glencoe, 1951), p. 15.
19. B. Malinowski, 'Culture', *Encylopaedia of Social Sciences* (New York, 1931) and Talcott Parsons, *op. cit.*, p. 15.
20. Compare F. Graebner, *Methode der Ethnologie* (Heidelberg, 1911) and G. Elliott Smith, *The Migration of Early Culture* (Manchester, 1929).
21. A. Etzioni and E. Etzioni (eds.), *Social Change* (New York, 1964), p. 80.
22. R. Linton, *The Study of Man* (London, 1936), p. 304.
23. G. P. Murdock, *Social Structure* (New York, 1949), p. 200.
24. See the earlier work of A. L. Kroeber, in his *The Nature of Culture* (Chicago, 1952), and the comment of David Bidney in *Theoretical Anthropology* (New York, 1953).
25. Talcott Parsons, 'The Roles of Ideas in Social Action', *American Sociological Review*, vol. III, no. 5, (1938).
26. Albert K. Cohen, *Delinquent Boys* (Glencoe, The Free Press, 1955).
27. Amitai Etzioni, *The Active Society* (New York, The Free Press, 1968), pp. 98–100, 432–454.
28. Milton M. Gordon, *Assimilation in American Life* (New York, Oxford University Press, 1964), p. 39.
29. *Ibid.*
30. See the chapter by A. E. Alcock in this volume for a different emphasis.
31. T. H. Bagley, *General Principles and Problems in the International Protection of Minorities* (Geneva, 1950), pp. 178 ff.
32. As for example, the combined difference of language *and* religion *and* ancient cultural heritage noted as a powerful attribute by L. Wirth. See his 'The Problem of Minority Groups' in R. Linton (ed.), *The Science of Man in the World Crisis* (New York, 1945), pp. 347–72.

33. Compare usage in R. A. Schermerhorn, *Comparative Ethnic Relations* (New York, Random House, 1970), pp. 125–7.
34. David O. Moberg, 'Social Differentiation in the Netherlands', *Social Forces*, vol. 39, no. 4 (May 1961), pp. 333–7.
35. Brian K. Taylor, 'The Challenge for Community Workers in Divided South Africa', *Community Development Journal*, vol. 12, no. 2 (1977), pp. 96–107.

2 The Present Position and Viability of Minority Languages

Glanville Price

The term 'minority language', as used in this chapter, denotes a language that is not merely spoken by only a minority of the population of a particular political unit but is in some way inferior in status to some other language or languages. In this connection, we shall make frequent use of the term 'diglossia', which was first given wide currency in an article by Charles A. Ferguson (1959).[1] For Ferguson, the term relates to communities in which 'two or more varieties of the same language are used by some speakers under different conditions', each variety 'having a definite role to play'. One of these varieties fulfils the functions of a superposed or H ('high') variety. It is 'learned largely by formal education and is used for most written and formal spoken purposes but is not used by any sector of the community for ordinary conversation'. The L ('low') variety is used in everyday conversation and other relatively informal contexts. The concept of diglossia has since been extended to include situations in which H and L are not varieties of the same language and in which H *is* the normal spoken medium of at least a section of the community;[2] this is the sense in which the term will be used here. One can usefully distinguish between diglossia and societal bilingualism, which occurs when two varieties fulfil approximately equivalent functions within a community, regardless of whether or not a substantial proportion of individuals are themselves bilingual.

The problems faced by minority languages are not peculiar to themselves. They arise primarily not from the fact that these are the languages of minority groups but from their sociolinguistic situation in relation to another language or languages. Many of the observations of Paul L. Garvin and Madeleine Mathiot

(1956)[3] on the Guaraní language, spoken by some 94 per cent of the population of Paraguay while Spanish is spoken by some 58·5 per cent, could be applied with little change in their essentials to some of the minority languages of western Europe.[4]

At the present time, the problem of minority languages is perhaps felt most acutely in western Europe where many such languages—including Basque, Catalan, Faroese, Frisian, Occitan, Romansh and all the remaining Celtic languages—are a subject of great concern, and these will be our main preoccupation.[5] It should not however be forgotten that similar problems arise, sometimes in the context of a multilingual rather than a bilingual community, in other parts of the world. In such circumstances, e.g. in Kenya and other parts of East Africa, there may be an 'in-group' language used for 'the basic face-to-face relationships with other speakers with whom the individual in question is fully identified', an 'out-group language' used 'for contacting people of groups outside their own community' and a 'language of specialised information' (e.g. English) used for such purposes as higher education or specialised formal training.[6] In this type of situation, the languages most at risk will be the 'in-group' languages, particularly in conditions in which one indigenous 'out-group' language, such as Swahili in Tanzania or Amharic in Ethiopia (as distinct from a 'language of wider communication' such as English, French or Spanish) is available to be fostered not only as an official language but as an instrument and a symbol of national identity.[7]

The problem of standardisation that faces many minority languages is one that also arises in relation to majority languages that, because of circumstances, are called on to be used in a wide range of functions in place of a hitherto dominant (and frequently alien) language (e.g., recently, Albanian).[8] However, the underprivileged status of many minority languages and the lack of established and authoritative institutions that might put their weight behind newly codified norms aggravates the problem. In some cases standardisation has become a major, and often a divisive, issue. In particular, the problem of dialectal variation can lead to acute differences of opinion as to whether the standard should be based firmly on one dialect (the unitary thesis) or whether an attempt should be made to select and blend elements from different dialects (the compositional thesis). For example, the various attempts made since the early nineteenth century with a view to codifying modern Occitan for literary purposes[9] have led to the establishment of two very different standardised varieties of the language, based on mutually exclusive principles (unitary and compositional respectively), and, regrettably, to a certain amount of antagonism between the supporters of the rival systems. Breton too has two orthographies and, although these do not differ as fundamentally as those that serve for the opposing varieties of Occitan, one sometimes sees time, effort and money that could better have been expended on effectively furthering Breton language and culture devoted to debate and occasionally dissension between partisans of the rival systems.

Romansh, now spoken by fewer than 50,000 people in the canton of Graubünden in eastern Switzerland, is characterised by marked dialectal fragmentation. The area is exceptionally mountainous and communications are difficult. Consequently, there was little to restrain the tendency towards separate development that inevitably manifests itself whenever a speech community is cut off from its neighbours. However, had there been any influential cultural or administrative centre in the Romansh area at the time when the language first came to be used for literary purposes, this might have helped to foster some degree of uniformity in the written language, but the capital of Graubünden, Chur, was germanised as early as the fifteenth century. Since the Reformation, distinct literary traditions have existed for Sursilvan in the west and two varieties of Engadinish in the east, and, in recent years, two central dialects, Sutsilvan and Surmiran, have also been standardised. Romansh therefore has at the moment five recognisably distinct written varieties. However, this tolerance of diversity has prevented the outbreak of quarrels such as those that have embittered relations in Occitania and Brittany.

Some minority languages on the other hand have succeeded in establishing generally acceptable norms in recent times. Examples are Faroese, which for over a century has used an etymologising orthography devised by V. U. Hammershaimb, and Catalan, for which the norms proposed by Pompeu Fabra in 1913 have been adopted—with modifications—by the *Institut d'Estudis Catalans* and may be considered authoritative, even though a problem remains in respect of Valencia and the Balearic Islands where there is resistance on the part of some to accepting without modifications the *Institut*'s norms which are based on the Catalan of Barcelona.[10]

The successful codification of a language is a major step, but, if it is not to be restricted in its functions to an unambitious range of topics, it must also acquire a word stock that is both flexible and precise enough to cope effectively with all the fields—literary, scholarly, technical, etc.—in which it is called on to serve.[11] In other words, there is a need for intellectualisation[12] and of elaboration.[13] A language may extend its vocabulary either by drawing on its own resources or by borrowing from other languages. In everyday contexts, a minority L language almost inevitably draws heavily on the corresponding H language. As a reaction against excessive borrowing from the H language in the everyday spoken language, those who are faced with the task of elaborating the vocabulary will often tend to indulge in systematic and perhaps excessive purism. The consequence is that the gap between the written and the spoken varieties may be much greater than is the case with certain other languages. This is all the more likely to be so when, as is often the case with minority languages, speakers thereof have been educated largely or wholly in the H language and so are unfamiliar with the vocabulary of many abstract, intellectual and technical registers of their own language. This may deepen the sense of inferiority that many of them have been conditioned to have about their own language and so alienate their sympathy.

There is a conflict here between two opposing tendencies. 'What modern language planners appear to be attempting is to achieve a proper balance between development of the language's own resources (which leads to purism) and responsiveness of the language to the world outside the community (which tempers purism and leads to greater acceptance of loanwords, particularly internationalisms)'.[14] It is clear that, at this stage in its development, the language may be manipulated by purists whereas later, when greater self confidence has been acquired, and the language's capacity to function as a modern idiom has been demonstrated, there will be less resistance to borrowings. 'Once anxiety over the functional capacity of the language is allayed, then the time may grow ripe for more sober linguistic considerations regarding efficiency, etc. of the code'.[15]

The dilemma facing those attempting to plan for the elaboration of the vocabulary of a minority language that is under considerable pressure from an H language of great prestige is that, if they do not resist the influx of foreign words, the native speakers may continue to feel—as many do—that it is inadequate for H functions. From this they are liable to generalise falsely and assume that it is intrinsically inferior, which in its turn hastens the process of what we might term 'alloglotticisation', of which specific examples are anglicisation in Wales, Ireland and Scotland, gallicisation in Brittany and other French provinces, germanisation in the Romansh valleys. On the other hand, if the language planners go for a native-based terminology and thereby widen the gulf between the spoken language and the written language, this too, as we have mentioned above, may have the effect of alienating the sympathy of ordinary speakers—i.e. the pursuit of a short-term objective (linguistic purism) may work against the achievement of the long-term aim (the salvation of the language).

OFFICIAL RECOGNITION

We now turn to consider the question of official recognition of minority languages and shall do so by taking a few examples by way of illustration. Since 1938, Romansh has been recognised in Switzerland not as an official language on a par with German, French and Italian, but as a national language. Consequently, although Romansh is not admissible in, for example, federal courts or in the citizen's dealings with the federal administration, federal subsidies are available for such purposes as the publishing of educational materials. Within the canton of Graubünden, however, Romansh is an official language along with German and Italian: in particular, proceedings in the cantonal courts and official business with the cantonal authorities may be transacted in the language. Nevertheless, in practice Romansh 'suffers serious disabilities (. . .) in the cantonal administration, and in the courts. Indeed, German is the main working language of the cantonal authorities.'[16]

The Welsh Language Act of 1967 represented a significant (if in some respects inadequate) step towards conferring official status on Welsh, by sanctioning and encouraging its use in legal proceedings and advocating its use in 'the conduct of other official or public business'. Consequently, various documents emanating from central and local government offices and other public bodies are now issued bilingually, bilingual road signs are gradually being introduced, and so on. To outward appearances, the situation of the language has improved dramatically. However, the reality behind the not unimpressive façade of 'official' Welsh is perhaps only slightly better than it was before. Ioan Bowen Rees comments thus on the situation as it was five years after the passing of the Welsh Language Act:

> In local government, Welsh is little used internally in writing and seldom used orally in formal debate or in presenting a case at a public inquiry: the government often appoint inspectors without a knowledge of Welsh to conduct inquiries in predominantly Welsh-speaking areas. Time and time again, a person who believes that a good citizen should use Welsh has to make a special point of asking for a Welsh version of a document, has to argue before the administration accept Welsh from him (. . .) Even when Welsh is available, he is seldom positively encouraged to use it.[17]

To this one might add that there is little evidence that Welsh-speakers avail themselves to any considerable extent of the opportunity that does now exist to use their language in many aspects of their dealings with public bodies. In practice, for many Welsh-speakers, English remains the H language for most purposes as German does for Romansh-speakers. Nevertheless, Welsh still enjoys much greater vitality than, say, Irish, and there may still be time for a general change in attitude that could establish Welsh in reality as well as in principle as a language for all purposes.

The 'Statute of Autonomy of Catalonia' of 1932 granted full recognition to Catalan (together with Spanish) as an official language in Catalonia. Under the Franco regime the language was banned from public life for some years and then allowed to be used only for certain limited and strictly cultural purposes. Many of the remaining restrictions on Catalan have recently been lifted and it seems likely that Catalan will not only soon become a fully official language again but that it will effectively function as such.

In France, although regional languages are under no kind of ban in the sense that they may be freely used in all non-official activities including the publishing of books and periodicals, they have no degree of official recognition whatsoever. Consequently, many Bretons and Occitans who regard their language as a *patois* rather than as a language worthy of respect are encouraged in this attitude by the manifest lack of respect in which regional languages are held by the authorities. There seems little hope in France of a declaration of the kind made in Spain in a decree of 31 October 1975 which, while reiterating the status of Castilian as sole official language, authorised the use of regional languages in all written and spoken media 'particularly in acts and meetings of a cultural nature' and recognised that 'the regional languages are a cultural heritage of the Spanish nation and all are regarded as national languages. Their knowledge and use will be assisted and protected by the action of the state and other public bodies.'

In the field of education too, the most illiberal policy is that followed in France. It was not until 1951 that the teaching of regional languages in state schools was allowed, and then only to a very limited extent and on such conditions as almost to nullify the positive provisions of the act except where there was considerable enthusiasm and a degree of self-sacrifice on the part of teachers, pupils and supporting bodies outside the schools. There has been significant improvement in recent years, but the situation is still not even minimally satisfactory.

Although it is too early to comment on the position of Catalan in state schools in Spain since the restoration of democracy, it is possible to report with some precision on the activities of private schools. A great deal has been done by a private organisation, *Omnium Cultural*, which in 1976–77 ran Catalan classes for some 227,000 children (three quarters of them from Castilian-speaking homes), and has also provided over a thousand teachers with training in the teaching of Catalan. Another movement, *Rosa Sensat*, has also, since 1965, been providing summer-schools and other training courses for Catalan teachers. With these foundations to build on, both the teaching of Catalan and education through the medium of Catalan can be expected to make considerable strides in the near future.

In Wales, much has been done in the last twenty or thirty years to set up primary schools—many of them in anglicised areas—where Welsh is the main medium of instruction, and a number of secondary schools where Welsh is the medium of instruction for many subjects and the normal working language of the school. In Graubünden, the language of instruction in primary schools is normally the majority language of the locality, but, in Romansh-speaking schools, German is gradually introduced, both as a subject and as a medium of instruction, and German is the medium of instruction in the secondary schools. However, the teaching of minority languages in schools and, more especially, their use as a medium of instruction raises a number of problems. It is sometimes difficult to secure specialists willing and qualified to teach certain subjects through a minority language; there is a shortage or absence of suitable text books for many subjects; it adds to costs to provide (as is now the case in many parts of Wales) a Welsh-medium or bilingual school as well as an English-medium school. There are also the social problems, and in particular a backlash against the teaching of a minority language on the part of those (some of them native speakers of the language) who argue that it is 'a waste of time' or 'a waste of money' or 'not in the best interests of the children'. The issue has become a socially divisive one in some parts of Wales. As all too often, it is difficult to find a solution that is not potentially damaging to the survival of a minority language. Not to press for a full role for it in the educational system is both to pay insufficient attention to one of the most powerful forces acting either for or against the language and to encourage the view that it is in some way inferior to the H language of the community. On the other hand, to press vigorously for the minority language to be given equal status with the H language in education is to run the risk of stirring up so much opposition and indeed hostility that, in the long run, the attempt may be counter-productive.

THREATS TO SURVIVAL

The mass media, with their all-pervasive influence, pose a threat of incalculable magnitude to the survival of minority languages. Breton, for example, has no newspapers, an hour a day at most on the radio, and one fifteen-minute programme a fortnight on television. Compared with this, Welsh is well endowed: there are no daily papers but two weeklies and numerous other magazines and journals, and programmes in Welsh occupy several hours a day on the radio, several hours a week on television. This is however very modest compared with the flood of English-language newspapers and other publications that are available, and of English-language radio and television programmes that easily and regularly penetrate into what was until some decades ago the Welsh-speaking heartland, comparatively free from anglicising influences. And this too, like education, is a socially divisive factor: for every Welsh programme occupying a slot on television, an English programme is displaced. So, whereas one section of the community argues that there is too little Welsh on television, others argue that there is too much. The creation of an all-Welsh channel has been urged from both sides. It has however been argued that, if this were done, many people who now watch Welsh programmes that are interspersed among other programmes would tend to leave their sets tuned to other channels and so watch even fewer Welsh programmes than at present.

Latest information about Catalan suggests that, as in many other respects, the situation has been completely transformed in the very recent past. Among the numerous periodicals is a daily paper, *Avui*, launched in 1976 and reported to have a circulation of some 50,000. One radio channel is now entirely given over to Catalan, but provision for Catalan on television averages only about an hour and a half a day, with nothing on Sundays or at peak viewing periods. The strength of Catalan in this as in other respects resides both in the very large number of speakers (probably between five and seven million) and in the degree of language loyalty demonstrated by its speakers.

Perhaps the most serious threat to an apparently well maintained language such as Catalan is that of immigration.[18] It appears that, whereas most native born inhabitants of Catalonia are Catalan-speaking, there is nevertheless a very high proportion of incomers who do not speak the language. According to Miquel Strubell i Trueta (1977),[19] these are mainly unskilled labourers who 'tend to be absorbed culturally within a couple of generations', the reason being 'basically, that Catalan enjoys high status in Catalonia'. He emphasises on the other hand that the smaller towns around Barcelona have been so much affected by the influx of hundreds of thousands of non-Catalan workers that they are now 'packed with Castilian speakers, leaving Catalans in a clear minority . . .', and in some areas 'most of the people' do not have Catalan as their everyday language. The consequence is that 'many second-generation immigrants are not getting the opportunity of learning the language'. Nevertheless, given the high status of Catalan, assimilation of the immigrants is apparently still regarded as feasible, provided the control of education is entrusted to an autonomous Catalan government.

The disastrous effect on a minority language of immigration brought about by industrialisation can also be illustrated from Wales where the sharp decline in the percentage of Welsh-speakers in the South Wales coalfield between 1901 and 1921 has been shown to be due, at least in part, to the immigration of workers from England.[20] In recent years, however, Welsh, and other languages including Scots Gaelic, Breton, Basque, Occitan and Romansh, have been threatened by a new type of immigration. The problem first arose in the mid-nineteenth century when relatively inaccessible areas where minority languages had been maintained were opened up to the outside world. Improved communications brought in tourists and, with them, alien tongues. Nowadays, tourism brings in money, leads to further improvement in communications, provides employment, and so is certainly of economic benefit. On the other hand, the material standard of living for the majority of the inhabitants of these areas remains appreciably lower than in the more affluent cities: 'The young Romansh people cannot be blamed if they go elsewhere in search of better-paid work, more congenial living conditions, greater opportunities for culture and entertainment, and shorter and more regular hours of work.'[21] Such areas may therefore suffer both from the social and cultural problems brought about by rural depopulation and from those arising from the immigration of people from the more affluent urbanised and industrialised areas who, in increasing numbers, are moving in either to retire or for leisure purposes. The settlement of substantial numbers of immigrants in what were until recently largely Welsh-speaking areas constitutes a serious threat to the survival of the language, and much the same is true in other minority language areas. This of course increases the likelihood of mixed marriages (e.g. marriages between Welsh-speakers and non-Welsh-speakers) which, it has recently been argued persuasively, can be shown to be a major factor in the decline of Welsh.[22] The same is doubtless true of other minority languages.

A recent survey[23] draws attention to some of the pressures put on underprivileged languages in modern industrialised and centralised societies which favour the expansion of standardised national languages to the detriment of minority languages, whose fate is summarised in the survey (p. 7) (not without some oversimplification) as follows:

> In a first stage their functions tend to be reduced to areas which are not directly concerned by 'modernization': rural traditions, religion, the private sphere. Further loss of functions then leads to language shift. . . . The mass media reinforce the geographical, social, and functional expansion of the national norms.

The same writers point out that members of linguistic minorities may 'internalize the bad connotations imposed on their group' and, in their fear of negative stereotypes and prejudices, experience identity conflicts and seek to avoid admitting membership of their group. This is well illustrated by the women of Bagnols-sur-Cèze, who, although Provençal is still widely spoken there, particularly by men, generally deny that they ever speak Provençal.

> They deny ever having learned or even having heard of it. If men try to introduce Provençal into family conversation, women forbid them to do so. They are very concerned that children learn correct French in order to prepare them well for school. . . . Apparently women are much more concerned about upward mobility than are men, and speaking correct French is a condition and symbol of the aspired status.[24]

A fundamental problem of language maintenance in the case of most minority languages is that, in general, there is no pressing economic, administrative or political necessity for the language to be maintained. Ben-Yehuda's efforts from the 1880s onwards to revive Hebrew as an everyday spoken language met with total success in less than a century, but two factors were present that are absent, or relatively weak, in the case of the languages with which we are concerned. One was the practical necessity of binding together into one community Jews from a wide variety of backgrounds. The other was that Hebrew had not one but many challengers, 'not one of which could claim to be known, even slightly, to everybody', so that it was 'abundantly clear . . . that, if Israel were not to become a second Tower of Babel, Hebrew would have to be the country's language, and all our newcomers would have to learn to use it in their daily lives'.[25] For speakers of minority languages, however, there is normally available another (usually only one other) language which not only *can* serve as the normal medium for all purposes but *does* so serve for some members of the community and which, as the H language in a diglossic situation, is often preferred for some purposes even by those whose home language is the L language. When the H language penetrates ever further into all spheres of social activity, the L language is increasingly less essential for purely utilitarian purposes. Its role is more and more that of serving as a symbol of identification for a given community. But when the desire for identification with a different—or wider—group becomes strong, it is understandable that symbols of identification with the minority may be abandoned.[26]

One has to ask whether, in increasingly industrialised and centralised societies, widespread personal bilingualism in a diglossic situation is not inevitably a stage on the way to ultimate alloglotticisation or shift of language. The realisation that this could be so has led in Wales to a campaign to define an area, based on that in which the majority of the inhabitants are Welsh-speaking, in which Welsh would be the sole or at any rate the principal language for official and other public purposes. The practical difficulties in the way of realisation of such a scheme do not seem to have been faced, least of all the likelihood that it would not appeal to a substantial proportion, perhaps a majority, of the Welsh-speakers themselves.

There seems little doubt that, though such factors as standardisation and official recognition can help, by conferring a degree of prestige, the decisive factor in determining the fate of a minority language is the degree of language loyalty shown by the community of speakers. If they continue to use it, it is likely to survive. Otherwise, it will die.

Circumstances seem propitious for the future of Catalan, but the chances of survival of many other minority languages must rest largely upon a change in attitudes. Given the increasing awareness in recent years of the social threats inherent in excessive centralisation in the economic, political, and cultural fields, and a reaction in favour of re-humanising society, it is too early to abandon hope. But time is very short and, the very special case of Hebrew notwithstanding, a dead language generally stays dead.

NOTES

1. C. A. Ferguson, 'Diglossia', *Word*, 15 (1959), pp. 325–40; reprinted in D.

Hynes (ed.), *Language in Culture and Society* (New York, 1964), pp. 429–39, and in P. P. Giglioli (ed.), *Language and Social Context* (Harmondsworth, 1972), pp. 232–51.

2. J. A. Fishman, 'Bilingualism with and without Diglossia; Diglossia with and without Bilingualism', *Journal of Social Issues* 23 (1967), pp. 29–38.
3. P. L. Garvin and M. Mathiot, 'The Urbanization of the Guarani Language: a Problem in Language and Culture' in A. F. C. Wallace (ed.), *Men and Culture* (Philadelphia, 1956), pp. 783–93; reprinted in Fishman (ed.), *Readings in the Sociology of Language* (The Hague, 1968), pp. 365–74.
4. W. Bright (ed.), *Sociolinguistics* (The Hague, 1971), pp. 277–93.
5. G. Price, *The Present Position of Minority Languages in Western Europe: A Select Bibliography* (Cardiff, 1969); supplements in *Orbis*, 21 (1972), pp. 235–47, and 25 (1976), pp. 162–75.
   G. Price, 'Minority Languages in Western Europe' in M. Stephens (ed.), *The Welsh Language Today* (Llandysul, 1973).
   M. Straka (ed.), *Handbuch der Europäischen Volksgruppen* (Vienna, 1970).
   S. Salvi, *Le Nazioni Proibite* (Florence, 1973).
   M. Stephens, *Linguistic Minorities in Western Europe* (Llandysul, 1976).
6. E. A. Nida and W. L. Wanderly, 'Communication Roles of Languages in Multilingual Societies' in W. H. Whiteley (ed.), *Language and Social Change in Problems of Multilingualism with Special Reference to Eastern Africa* (Oxford, 1971), pp. 57–74.
7. J. A. Fishman, 'National Languages and Languages of Wider Communication in the Developing Nations', in W. H. Whiteley (ed.), *op. cit.*
8. J. L. Byron, *Selection Among Alternates in Language Standardisation: The Case of Albanian* (The Hague, 1976).
9. G. Price, 'The problem of Modern Literary Occitan', *Archivum Linguisticum*, 16 (1964), pp. 34–53.
   G. Kremnitz, *Versuche zur Kodifizierung des Okzitanischen seit dem 19. Jh. und ihre Annahme durch die Sprecher* (Tübingen, 1974).
10. E. Haugen, 'Linguistics and Language Planning' in W. Bright (ed.), *op. cit.*
   J. A. Fishman, 'Language Modernisation and Planning in Comparison with Other Types of National Modernisation and Planning', *Language in Society*, 2 (1973), pp. 23–43.
   J. A. Fishman, 'Language Planning and Language Planning Research: The State of the Art', in J. A. Fishman (ed.), *Advances in Language Planning* (The Hague, 1974), pp. 15–53.
11. P. L. Garvin (tr.), 'General Principles for the Cultivation of Good Language', in J. Rubin and R. Shuy (eds.), *Language Planning: Current Issues and Research*, (Washington, D.C., 1973), pp. 102–11; reprinted in J. A. Fishman *op. cit.* (1974), pp. 417–26.
12. See Bohuslav Havranek quoted in Garvin and Mathiot, *op. cit.*
13. E. Haugen, 'Dialect, Language, Nation', *American Anthropologist*, 68 (1966), pp. 922–35; reprinted in *Studies by Einor Haugen* (The Hague, 1972), pp. 296–509.
14. Byron, *op. cit.*, p. 124.
15. *Ibid.*, p. 125.
16. K. D. McRae, *Switzerland. Example of Cultural Coexistence* (Toronto, 1964), p. 14.

17. I. B. Rees, 'The Welsh Language in Government', in M. Stephens, *op. cit.* (1973), p. 215.
18. R. Ninyoles, *Cuatro Idiomas Para Un Estado* (Madrid, 1977), especially Chapter V, 'Los Immigrantes y su Integración Lingüistica', pp. 111–46.
19. M. Strubell i Trueta, 'Catalunya—Back in the Running After the Recent Elections in Spain', *Planet*, no. 39 (August 1977), pp. 2–7.
20. J. G. Thomas, 'The Geographical Distribution of the Welsh Language' in *Geographical Journal*, no. 122 (1956), pp. 71–9.
21. A. Widmer, 'Das Ratoromanische in Graubünden', *Orbis*, 14 (1966), pp. 560–71.
22. D. B. Scully, 'Marriage Patterns and the Decline of Welsh', *Planet*, no. 40 (November 1977), pp. 8–10.
23. W. Dressler, and R. Wodak-Leodolter (eds.), 'Language Death' in *International Journal of the Sociology of Language*, no. 12 (The Hague, 1977), pp. 5–11.
24. B. Schlieben-Lange, 'The Language Situation in Southern France' in Dressler and Wodak-Leodolter, *op. cit.*, pp. 104–5.
25. E. Elath, *Hebrew and the Jewish Renaissance* (Leeds, 1961), p. 15.
26. B. Schlieben-Lange, *op. cit.*

3 Comparative Perspectives on the Education of Cultural Minorities

Margaret B. Sutherland

Education is traditionally held to be a process by which the social heritage is transmitted: a society passes on by formal teaching those aspects of its knowledge, skills, way of life which it wishes to perpetuate. The main problems in the education of cultural minorities arise when the transmission of these elements by a minority appears to conflict with the transmission of the skills and values of the major social group; or when the minority lacks the resources to provide formal education for its children and needs help from the majority. The problems are acute when the dominant group regards education in patriotism or its own ideology as essential; in such cases, the transmission of other values or loyalties by the majority appears as a threat. But reasons of expediency may also lead a dominant social group to disregard the wishes of a minority group and impose a common education. For example, there is greater administrative simplicity if all schools employ the same language of instruction, follow the same curriculum, use the same textbooks. The recruitment and education of teachers are also simplified in such conditions. Children can be gathered in common schools of reasonable size rather than in what are—from the economic point of view—excessively small units. Much of course depends on the amount of centralisation of control of education found in a given country; but provision for minority groups does not necessarily correspond with the amount of local control permitted in the educational system of a country.

THE MINORITY'S ATTITUDE TO EDUCATION

A minority group's attitude to education depends greatly on its perception of its own status. This perception is affected by the frame of reference—neighbourhood, regional, national or world: for example, French speakers may be in a minority within a given country but feel themselves part of a numerically strong group—the Francophones—on the world scale; Jews may be in a minority in one area yet feel the reassurance of membership of a major group, the Jewish people. There may also be a conflict of perceptions when different rights are concerned; Afrikaans-speaking white South Africans are in a majority position in the government of the country but in a threatened minority position so far as the Afrikaans language is concerned.

Also of major importance for education is the group's evaluation of those elements which give it its identity—principally its history, way of life, religion, language. A cultural minority may regard all these as vital to its existence; but it is also possible for the minority to consider only one or two essential and to accept that the others may be changed or relinquished. The group may be willing to become assimilated to some extent: it may wish its children to acquire some of the characteristics of the surrounding society—e.g., language—which can have great utility value, but insist on keeping the defining characteristic of the minority religion. Thus in some cases parents are not enthusiastic about the provision of schools which will apparently 'protect' the minority group by teaching in its home language; from the parental point of view, this may be a way of blocking their children's advancement in later employment—for instance, it is claimed that in the eighteenth and nineteenth centuries, Scottish Gaelic speakers were by no means anxious that their children should be schooled in Gaelic; African parents may likewise be resentful of home-language teaching instead of 'world language' teaching. In some instances, e.g., Welsh, there may be controversy within the cultural group as to whether the language *is* an essential characteristic (the introduction of Welsh-medium or bilingual schools has not been universally welcomed by Welsh parents).

Alternatively, there may be little concern about the religious atmosphere of schools but different groups may cherish the provision of education in their own language—as, for example in Malaysia. In Singapore, some Chinese groups accept English-medium schools whereas others feel strongly in favour of Chinese-medium schools as a means of ensuring the survival not only of language but of way of life. Thus it is a matter of importance to distinguish what, in the opinion of a minority group are its distinctive characteristics; and to recognise the attitude of the group towards at least partial assimilation through education. At one extreme of the assimilation continuum would come such cases as that of the Japanese *burakumin* or 'unemancipated communities' whose group characteristic is that ancestors were engaged in 'outcast' occupations some centuries ago and the descendants are still socially outcast. Here the group itself has urged on the government special efforts to produce assimilation in the rest of Japanese society; such a group seeks to lose its separate identity and looks to education as a means to this end.

Attitudes towards acceptance of the school system of the majority society also depend greatly on the confidence of the minority group in its ability to transmit its language, religion or culture by the influences of the home and neighbourhood; e.g., religion may be—in the view of the group—effectively transmitted by family and other out-of-school religious observances. In such cases, the formal school system of the majority group is looked on as neutral or positively beneficial in giving necessary skills while leaving intact the essential characteristics of the minority. Possibly in such cases minority groups fail to recognise the insidious influences of the 'hidden curriculum' of schools—the attitudes conveyed by the materials of school teaching and the school's own way of life; such influences may be inimical to the group's culture, though not overtly so. Occasionally one does find a minority group realisation of such a possible influence—e.g., the Muslim parents' protest in Bradford against the provision of coeducational schools for their daughters.

On the practical level, for full-time or part-time minority education, much depends on the wealth of the minority group and its numerical strength within a neighbourhood. If the country's educational system allows private schools, a minority group of fair wealth and with a moderately dense distribution within an area is able to establish its own schools, with its own kind of education. Where the group is thinly scattered, as, e.g., the minority group of Protestants in the Republic of Ireland, residential education may have to be provided—if the group can afford this or if the majority government is willing to give financial aid.

There is, in contemporary society, a conflicting factor in the demand for provision of education for minority groups. In some instances allocation of the children of the minority group to a special school or special classes (e.g., immigrant children learning English) may be viewed as an instance of negative discrimination. The minority group may feel that if its children are not receiving the same education as the children of the majority group, an attempt is being made to depress the status of the minority. Hence the valiant if unrewarded efforts in the United States to ensure, by the unpopular bussing policy, that black American children are visibly in precisely the same classrooms as whites.

THE MAJORITY'S ATTITUDE TO EDUCATION

From the majority point of view, the provision of special education for minority groups depends greatly on majority feelings of strength or weakness. Thus some countries tolerate religious differences but find language differences unacceptable. In others, language differences may be acceptable—as in primary education in the USSR—while religious teaching is unacceptable. It is presumably a sign of confidence in the position of the French language that the French government agreed in 1951 to concede a difference strongly opposed earlier—the optional teaching of possible rivals to the French language (Basque, Occitan, for example) in primary school classes in France.

But the major argument expressed by politicians against minority education is the socially divisive effect of separate schools. It has been claimed—for instance in France after the Franco-Prussian War—that common schools for all children of a country will have the effect of developing civic consciousness and a feeling of national unity; the Nazis had a similar view. Separate schools, it is argued, lead to the formation of separate groups, having a loyalty to their own distinctive political or religious creed which will inevitably weaken the structure of society and lessen the harmony of civic life. On a simpler level, children attending the same school as those belonging to other cultural groups will get to know the members of these groups, to form friendships with them and thus avoid accepting stereotypes based on hearsay, lack of experience, ignorance, which can lead to later hostility and aggression within society. (Note, for instance, the call for 'integrated' schools in Northern Ireland at present.) Similarly, the use of the same textbooks throughout all schools will ensure common views of history, shared enjoyment of the same cultural heritage.

On the level of expediency, if a manpower planning policy is in operation, central control of access to vocational education and higher education is desirable; such education may therefore be best provided within one system of schools only.

Educational provision for minority groups therefore depends on a multitude of inter-related factors both of cultural values and of administrative and economic considerations. It is affected by the majority group's estimate of its own position and future as well as by the minority group's self-perception and wishes. The ways in which these factors operate and the problems for which solutions have been sought may be better understood if we look at some of the policies adopted in different educational systems.

POLICIES FOR THE TEACHING OF RELIGION

One of the common requirements of minority groups is provision for the teaching of their characteristic religion. Here, policies range from total refusal to provide for distinctive religious teaching in schools to total acceptance of the need to provide such schools.

At one extreme, that of total refusal to incorporate distinctive religious teaching in the schools of the country, we find examples in the USSR and the USA. In the USSR, while parents are free to practise their own religion and to instruct children in it, and while there is some state acceptance of seminaries for the training of priests of the orthodox Church, all children must attend the same schools and no school provision of religious teaching is permitted—schools indeed have the duty of inculcating anti-religious views, pointing out to children the superstitious nature of religion and its outmoded bourgeois qualities. It is noteworthy that, given this situation, various religious groups have succeeded in maintaining their distinctive culture, greatly as their numbers may have been depleted at various times.

The position in the USA has been more fluid in respect of the teaching of religion in schools. While lessons characteristic of religious creed are unconstitutional in public schools, it is legitimate in the USA to establish private denominational schools; and this the Catholic Church and other religious groups have done. There has also been in the USA, since the Second World War, a gradual provision of some financial aid from public funds for such schools—not as direct subsidies but as fringe benefits, welfare benefits. So minority groups are catered for; though it is misleading in some ways to talk of the Roman Catholic population as a minority group, since they predominate in certain urban districts. Further, Catholic minority groups may differ from each other according to their country of origin—the interpretation of Catholicism of Irish settlers may not be that of Polish or of Mexican settlers. Linguistic and cultural differences complicate the situation so that it would be erroneous to suggest that giving religious teaching necessarily provides fully for the cultural education distinctive of the groups; though where the teachers come from the same area as the pupils and share the same parental language, the school may indeed reinforce not only the religious teaching of the home but also its culture. Nevertheless the public school system of the USA has the clear intention of fostering common loyalty among the different groups (witness the flag-saluting of the classroom); it insists on the acquisition and use of the common language; and, on the whole, minority groups tend to accept such assimilative procedures.

It is also to be remarked that in the USA attempts have been made to discover by empirical evidence whether the assertions commonly made about the effects of separate Church schools have substance. Using the admirable conditions for experiment resulting from the availability of Church and public school and college systems, A. M. Greeley and P. H. Rossi's study, 'The Education of Catholic Americans' (National Opinion Research Centre Monograph, Chicago, 1966), tried to establish whether attendance at public or Church schools and colleges did in fact produce social divisiveness and firm adherence to the Catholic Church. The results proved capable of a variety of interpretations; but essentially it appeared that there was not evidence of a divisive effect—people did tend to associate with those of their own religious group as friends but this was true also of those who went through the 'integrated' public school system; private system graduates were as involved as public in community affairs; and becoming a good practising Catholic appeared to depend on home and marriage influences rather than on the type of school attended. 'Minority' schools thus neither protected the survival of the minority group nor harmed the majority.

In France also there has been flexibility which has lately led to the provision of some public financial support for schools (mainly Roman Catholic) in the 'private' sector. This is noteworthy since

France also decided, originally at the Revolution, then again in the 1880s, that education in the public schools should be secular, religious education being left to parents to ensure; Thursday indeed was left free as a day on which this could be done. Religious orders were forbidden, at the beginning of this century, to conduct schools. But the freedom given to private citizens to establish schools meant that in practice the religious orders continued to provide education and very considerable numbers of children have attended these schools rather than the public schools. The feeling that a minority group is being discriminated against if it has to pay fees for its children's education while public schools are free seems to have led to the Debré Law of 1959 which introduced a system of contracts according to which denominational schools conforming to certain requirements concerning curriculum and teacher qualifications can receive financial resources necessary for running the schools. It must be recognised that this development has not been unopposed—there are indeed still demands that the private sector should be closed down.

In England and in Northern Ireland a similar compromise of considerable public financial support for denominational schools (in England, about half of these are Anglican) evolved much earlier, the amount of support increasing recently from 65 per cent to approximately 85 per cent. In Northern Ireland, while almost all the 'voluntary' schools at primary and secondary intermediate (or secondary modern) level provide for the Roman Catholic minority, at secondary level the situation is complicated by the fact that many of the voluntary grammar schools thus aided by public funds are not intended to give denominational education (or other special minority group culture education): most of those catering mainly for Protestant pupils have origins other than in a religious foundation. In these cases, however, it must be noted that provision for the special needs of minority groups does seem to run counter to one of the current educational demands—that for comprehensive education; wholehearted supporters of the 'comprehensive' ideal find it hard to accept segregation of parts of the population.

In other countries, minority group preferences for distinctive religious education in schools have been safeguarded by separate administrative provision. In Quebec province, Canada, where the Catholic/French-speaking group is strong, there has been an officially dual system, schools being under the control of Protestant Boards or of Catholic Boards; parity of conditions has thus been ensured as far as possible but the situation has been so complicated by language and other cultural factors that the ideal solution of the problem has clearly not yet been found. In Newfoundland, where divisions of a cultural kind do not complicate the issue, three boards representing different religious affiliations are found—the Catholic, the Integrated (i.e., Anglican and other Protestant), and the Pentecostal. The function of the boards is to make proposals for additional schools as required and of course to ensure the appropriate religious instruction and staff appointments in schools under their jurisdiction. But the provincial Ministry of Education is responsible for all other aspects of the schools—e.g., finance, curriculum—and minority group feelings do not seem to lead to tensions; indeed when schools are overcrowded parents may try to enter their children in a school across the religious line, to avoid a bus journey for the child.

In Scotland the provision for minority religious schools has been simplified by the 1918 Act under which the Roman Catholic schools have become part of the public system, the Church authorities handing over their schools to the local education authorities but retaining the right to ensure and supervise the continuing provision of religious education and to approve the appointment of suitable teachers (i.e., of the appropriate faith) to the school. There are, occasionally, allegations that this system creates or enhances social tensions between Catholics and Protestants; but in the areas where such tensions may be found—i.e., mainly in the big city areas of Glasgow and Dundee—it would be difficult to assess the influence of the school as distinct from the home and neighbourhood situation. There are at present, as in some other countries, practical problems of staffing Catholic schools appropriately in some subject areas and this has created uneasiness as to the opportunities offered to pupils in, e.g., mathematics; but the most recent changes in the teacher supply situation may well eliminate this problem.

Looking at minority groups' wishes for religious education of a characteristic kind we thus find a variety of provisions to meet these wishes. There are also some indications that the demand for such provisions is less strong today than in times past. In the nineteenth century the attempt in Ireland to provide non-denominational National Board schools for all children failed because of the hostility shown by parents and churchmen, both

Catholic and Protestant. Possibly, in various countries there might now be more tolerance of 'mixed' schooling though some parents would certainly still consider that religious teaching must permeate the whole school day and thus cannot adequately be given in a school catering for various denominations. But for others the right of withdrawing from religious education if the parent wishes the child not to attend (a right recognised in the UK and other Western countries—indeed, in West Germany, the *pupil* has the right to decide, after age 14, whether to attend religious lessons or not) would seem sufficient safeguard.

If parents were ready for such acceptance a practical problem might be solved for provision for minority groups can create a large number of small schools—in Germany, picturesquely known as 'dwarf' schools (*Zwergschulen*). In rural areas, in Northern Ireland for example, one finds in close proximity one-teacher or two-teacher schools of different religious backgrounds dealing with a wide age-range—possibly with the whole primary age-range. This problem can of course arise also if separate provision is made according to language preferences but that factor seems to have been less active in producing such a situation. While one-teacher or two-teacher schools can have advantages it would often be better educationally for the children if the school populations were combined in a larger primary school with greater resources in staffing, equipment, etc. Similarly at secondary level a combined school could offer pupils better facilities and a greater choice of subjects. These educational considerations have to be weighed against minority group preferences.

Yet a point of major importance to the existence of cultural minority groups may explain the anxiety still felt by many parents about schools which mix young people of different religious beliefs; it is anxiety about future intermarriage. This anxiety has been particularly strong in communities where the religious division has been on Protestant-Catholic lines. Protestants especially have worried about the ruling of the Catholic Church that the children of a mixed marriage should be educated as Catholics; the recent relaxation of this rule by Catholic bishops in England should produce a notable reduction of tension. Where tensions between groups are strong, this particular aspect gains in importance in Northern Ireland at present, when partners in a mixed marriage may find themselves the object of special hostility or suspicion in their neighbourhood or community the anxiety (which had perhaps been diminishing in the 1960s) is reinforced. Similar concerns are evident in the attitude of parents in London and other areas of England where ethnic and religious groups mix in schools; parents of Hindu girls, for example, give firm warnings against friendship with Sikh or white boys. It is true that future marriages are more a matter of out-of-school life; but the mixed school is seen as giving opportunities which would not otherwise occur (given the segregation of groups in out-of-school life) for forming undesirable attachments. What is seen by some educators as a great advantage of the 'mixed' school, the development of better understanding between different groups, is seen as a disadvantage by parents who would not wish tolerance to go to the lengths of intermarriage.

Similarly, parents may fear that in the 'mixed' school children will receive opinions about their roles which are contrary to those of their own religious or cultural teaching; thus, for example, a school which encourages girls to make their own decisions about their future career and marriage may be in opposition to the home religious teaching which makes it the role of women to be obedient to parents and to husband, leaving decisions to be taken by others. Marriage is regarded as a matter of such importance that it cannot be left to the individual judgment of the girl or boy. Hence, conscientious school counsellors, anxious both to respect the difference in culture of minority groups and to maintain the rights of the individual pupil find themselves in a particularly trying dilemma. Marriage is the way in which a group perpetuates itself; within the family unit the way of life—language, religion, morals, customs—of the group is maintained and propagated. An educational system which aims at changing the attitudes of young people—or which simply offers them examples within school of a different set of attitudes—offers a threat to the maintenance of the minority group culture. One can understand that the parents of a minority group may prefer the sheltered environment of a school giving their own distinctive religious formation in a group of like-minded teachers and pupils.

POLICIES FOR LANGUAGE OF INSTRUCTION

Minority groups may in some instances find the religious factor subordinate to the linguistic factor as an assertion of their identity and therefore be more concerned about the latter. In Belgium, for example, though the population is largely Roman Catholic, at least nominally, there has been a clear division between Flemings (Dutch-speaking) and Walloons (French-speaking) with regard to the provision of religious education in schools, the former supporting denominational schools: it was only in 1958 that the Education Pact established equal conditions for both denominational and secular schools. But the conflict to establish both languages as having equal status has continued and the present solution of having education within defined parts of the country either by the medium of French or of Dutch (or in a limited eastern area, German) while acceptable has not yet reduced the tensions—as witness the strong opposition to the proposed extension of the University of Louvain (French-speaking section) into what was technically Dutch-language territory. Provision has also been made in Brussels, with its often bi-lingual population, for children to attend schools using the medium of their home language.

But the provision of schools using the home language as medium of instruction does not always satisfy minority group feelings. The French-speaking minority in Canada has until recently felt its language to be neglected and given inferior status; federal government policy has now moved to official bi-lingualism and although education is a matter of provincial government responsibility federal aid has been given to help provinces to improve the teaching of French in their schools. But in the province of Quebec where, as we have noted, separate boards exist to provide for the Catholic and Protestant populations, a French-speaking majority has now ruled that children must attend schools using the language of their home. This deprives parents of freedom of choice: and as in fact attendance at English-language schools is permitted only if at least one parent has received education for at least three years of primary school in an English-language Quebec school or if the child has a sibling already attending such a school, the ruling causes much dissatisfaction—especially as those moving into Quebec, and immigrants from other countries, are thus bound to send their children to French-language schools. Thus administrative interpretations of 'home language' can be tendentious. This attempt to relieve the pressures on an 'oppressed minority' (in the national context) results in English-speakers in the province feeling like an oppressed minority. Oddly enough, the attempt to solve the language problem by schools with parallel streams, using different languages as media of instruction, though tried in some countries, does not seem to survive long: nor does the attempt, as made briefly in South Africa, to have the teacher bi-lingual, saying everything in two languages.

In contrast to some of the minority provisions already mentioned the example of Jewish education in Britain gives indications of the way in which parents of a minority group provide for the maintenance of their characteristic religion, language and way of life while adapting largely to the majority group. The Jewish group can provide for its children in denominational state-aided schools on the basis already noted with regard to Catholic and Anglican schools. In fact, some 21 per cent of British Jewish children attend primary and secondary Jewish day schools, which vary in the proportion of the curriculum given to distinctively Jewish studies; and of the 57 schools in this group, 20 are state-aided. A very small number of Jewish children attend private Jewish schools (*yeshivot*), in which the curriculum is centred on Jewish studies and the staff are all observant Jews. But for the majority of Jewish school children who receive any distinctively Jewish education (and it has been estimated that 30 per cent do not receive such education) the common pattern is attendance at ordinary schools supplemented by attendance at special schools (teaching religious knowledge, some Hebrew and Jewish history) during out-of-school time. It has been estimated that 49 per cent of Jewish children are educated in this way. Another form of out-of-school education—youth clubs—may also be effective in providing learning about the Jewish race and religion and mixing with those of the same culture group, but some youth clubs appear rather to help in assimilation in the surrounding culture. In some ways a similar pattern may be developing for immigrant populations in England where attendance at ordinary schools is being supplemented by attendance at classes in the group's own language and religion, e.g., by Muslim children. The formal organisation of regular classes in out-of-school time seems to serve both the practical purpose of transmitting religion and/or language and that of strengthening consciousness of membership of the cultural minority group. Such activities serve to make both the minority and the majority groups aware of the differences between them: and to demonstrate parents' concern for their culture.

Although language rather than religion may be the distinctive feature of a minority group one can understand the motives which lead a majority government to insist on education through a common, majority language. In the USSR, the acceptance of the home language for the first classes of primary school, when the language is one spoken by a relatively small group, followed by using Russian as the medium of study is easily comprehensible. One can also recognise the need in newly independent African countries to choose a common language rather than educate in a number of individual tribal languages—though again, provision may have to be made, for a length of time not yet perhaps finally decided, for teaching initially in the home language. (Teacher supply problems make such teaching sometimes difficult to ensure.) Similarly one can recognise the fluctuations of feeling as to choice of a common language and the lingering resentment against the 'majority' languages of English or French which leads to decisions such as that of Tanzania to opt rather for Ki-Swahili. But in other instances, the reason for choice of a common language in the face of minority groups' wishes is less easily justifiable. In Malaysia where the population of a number of racial groups has been catered for by schools using Chinese, Malay, Tamil and other Indian languages, a decision has now been made that Malay shall be the language of instruction for all groups. Yet Singapore, while providing much the same language groups, has opted rather for a bi-lingual policy, English being required either as the medium of instruction or as a second language. It should be noted that where minority groups have the possibility of taking primary and secondary education through their own language they may have problems in finding higher education through it—e.g., it is only recently that Chinese speakers have had a university (Nanyang) using Mandarin as the medium of instruction: Tamil speakers still lack such a facility.

Certainly the effects of imposing a language can be educationally undesirable. In Hong Kong where English has been taught alongside the home language (mainly Cantonese) in the primary school but has been essential for success in the examination for entry to secondary education, and in secondary school has been the medium of instruction, the majority group's education has been dominated by a minority language which is often imperfectly mastered and which leads to inadequate learning or study methods. The situation also exacerbates group resentments. Yet it does not seem as if the cultural identity of the Chinese-speaking groups has been threatened or diminished by this policy, out-of-school influences being certainly strong enough to prevent such effects. The ineffectiveness of the imposed 'other language' is instanced again in the South African situation for White South Africans where both the official languages of the country have to be studied in schools. The medium of instruction is however the home language; and despite the availability of books, journals, broadcasts in the 'other' language the two groups remain remarkably constant in the use of their own language—and indeed tend to keep to social groups using their own language.

The South African situation does however also illustrate the burden of language learning where minority languages have to be safeguarded. The Bantu or African child, educated initially in the home language, must also learn both the official languages. A further illustration of the extra language burden comes from the Indian situation where, to meet with the immense number of languages in the country while satisfying group and national feelings, the 'three language formula' has been devised; by this children have to learn Hindi, the national language; English as a valuable second language; and those whose home language is Hindi or English are supposed to learn a third language so as to maintain equality with those children whose home language is not Hindi or English.

Nonetheless, the use or study of a language often is used as a symbol of the assertion of identity of a minority group. Within the British Isles—and even within Scotland's separate system of education—Scottish nationalism has not been able to use language as a rallying point since Gaelic has not been the language of all Scots and since the proposal of Lallans as 'the' Scottish language had no hope of succeeding (being incomprehensible to many Scots and not the home language of any). But Welsh, which is the home language of many though not of a majority of Welsh people, now seems to be used more effectively as a rallying symbol. There has since 1947 been a development of Welsh schools and bi-lingual schools; but this is a matter of decision by local education authorities, who might be expected to adapt to local needs and wishes, rather than central government policy—though the powers in education given to the Welsh Office in 1970 could be regarded as a decision by the British Government to recognise Welsh minority group rights. It remains to be seen whether the influence of the schools where Welsh is used will be strong enough to expand the use of the language as a characteristic of the whole cultural group.

The Irish example would seem to be, on the whole, discouraging as an instance of an attempt to strengthen cultural group identity through a characteristic language. Despite governmental policy in the Republic of Ireland in making the Irish language compulsory as a subject of study, the proportion of Irish speakers has remained small. One must recognise again the importance of the out-of-school situation in the life of a language; and the vital difference between teaching a language in schools and using the language as the medium of instruction. Few children (except those in the *Gaeltacht*) hear the language spoken in everyday life, and the language has been taught in schools as a separate subject—in almost all cases—and indeed often taught almost as a dead language: so it is not really astonishing that it has not become an essential part of life for those who otherwise feel themselves certainly Irish. Similar problems have beset the teaching of Irish in the Northern Ireland schools. Here the study of the subject has certainly been a claim to characteristic identity by the minority Roman Catholic group. The freedom left to schools in the UK generally to choose which subjects are to be taught (and examined) has made it possible for Roman Catholic schools to opt for the Irish language while other schools have offered other modern or ancient languages. But again Irish has been taught—sometimes with inadequate textbooks and methods—as another subject on the timetable, studied for reasons of cultural heritage, possibly, but from the point of view of the learners not useful for everyday communication: and indeed, especially when combined with Latin, blocking the chance of learning a language like French or German which might have more utility value. So that although the language has served as symbol of minority group membership, its use has not become characteristic of the group. (It should be noted that for many Northern Irish Protestants the study of Irish is attractive also as an affirmation of the Irish nationality which they feel themselves to have; though it is not generally offered to them in school, it remains an attractive study in adult education.)

POLICIES FOR OTHER ASPECTS OF THE CURRICULUM

Thus religion and language of minority culture are included in the school system of at least some countries. Variations to suit minority group interest in other aspects of the curriculum are less frequent. In the majority of countries the content of the curriculum is centrally determined or at least under the control of a local education authority: similarly the textbooks are either centrally determined or have to be chosen from lists approved by the central educational authority or its representatives. The freedom enjoyed by UK schools to determine subjects to be included in the curriculum, the content of these subjects and the choice of books is decidedly exceptional. In most systems it is only in private schools—where these are permitted—that the curriculum can differ largely from that of the public schools of the country. Moreover, where success in a public, externally controlled examination is important to the learners, the content of what is taught in schools will be adjusted to suit these examination requirements; hence, even schools which are private or use a language which is not that of the majority group will tend to present the same information to their pupils. Even so, some subject areas will provide opportunities for teaching minority group culture. Probably the most fertile area for such cultural development is in literature and language; the choice of texts in the minority group language can do much to reinforce cultural awareness. In the teaching of literature, poetry, music, minority group membership may be strengthened; assuming, that is, that the allegedly characteristic language itself is not a barrier to comprehension and enjoyment.

There is also considerable scope for cultural development in the less formal subjects of the school curriculum, in music, crafts, dance and art. Unhappily in very many systems these are somewhat neglected areas of school work, where teacher competence is poor. In the primary school, if curriculum content is not prescribed in detail, much cultural information may be imparted by story-telling, by imaginative play, by the treatment of social studies (history, geography).

The subject of history is of special interest since this presents to the new generation knowledge of the past of its own group. It is thus an area in which central government control of studies may be particularly firm or in which great public interest may be shown (witness the discussions in East and West Germany of the amount and kind of attention given in school texts to the history of the Nazi period). It has been argued that in the UK minority group rights have been infringed by the tendency of history books to deal with history from the English point of view—that Scottish children may learn Scottish history up to 1603 but thereafter approach the topic from an English point of view; Northern Ireland children in the controlled schools learn, it is suggested, English or British history, remaining ignorant of Irish history or finding events in Ireland referred to only incidentally as they impinged on English history. In the Roman Catholic schools in Northern Ireland the presentation of history is said to have been different; certainly some research on knowledge of present-day political personages would suggest that the two groups of children lived in different historical settings. It should be noted that while in many countries schools may be constrained by official curricula or by the examination system—pupils and teachers there knowing that to obtain success or stand up to inspectors' visits the 'correct' interpretation of history must be given. This does not apply in the British examination system, where it is easy to avoid certain periods of history, or even the subject of history altogether. But in any system the gloss put upon the teaching of history by the teacher in the classroom is beyond official control (unless by unusually constant monitoring by others in the school): teachers and pupils can enter on an implicit or explicit understanding as to what is 'true' history and what is to be offered for public inspection.

This kind of transmission by the time-honoured oral method may be more effective than book-learning of history, especially when it is reinforced by family and neighbourhood beliefs. Evidence concerning it is naturally difficult to obtain; but informal reports suggest that it happens for various minority groups. It is also evident in this context how important it is for the minority group to have teachers belonging to the group, if culture and history are to be transmitted as the group would wish. At the same time, such a shared group membership could reinforce a ghetto mentality which is not educationally desirable.

Further, in many countries more international interpretations of history are being sought. UNESCO has fostered various studies to compare the presentation of history within different countries and to produce textbooks giving a more balanced picture of events so that children educated in different countries will not receive radically different versions. In Scandinavia, collaboration between the different countries has led to general agreement on the presentation of history in schools. Such trends might aid the preservation of minority group cultures if they produced a fairer picture of historical events; but at the same time they militate against the individual bias in interpretation which may characterise either national or minority group teaching of history.

PROBABLE EFFECTS OF EDUCATION ON MINORITY GROUPS

Finally, one must ask what are the probable effects on minority groups of present attitudes in education. We have already noted some points where general educational principles do not favour minority group education. In many countries however there is now a strong belief in the need to respect minority cultures and to make all members of the population knowledgeable about them and tolerant of them; hence attempts to teach about different religions, ethnic beliefs, customs; hence efforts—in the USA, UK and Scandinavia—to reform school books to prevent an ethnocentric or chauvinist bias. But the effect of such teaching must surely be to make minority cultures more self-conscious in a way which, though producing pride in membership, may simultaneously lead the individual to support the culture artificially; customs may be maintained not because that is how one naturally lives but because this is the behaviour which other people expect. (One sees such developments in the tourist trade.) There may be, too, a reaction by the majority group, a questioning as to how far majority culture can accommodate to minorities without imperilling its own characteristics.

There is also the question of the general aim of education in schools. In many countries, it is accepted that education should produce the individual who is capable of rational judgment, making an individual choice as to religion and the way of life to be followed. Modern means of communication reinforce awareness of alternative values and ways of life. Thus the product of education, even one whose minority rights in religion and language have been respected may question the basis of membership in the minority group, the origins of the group and the value of its beliefs. Language can remain as a means of communication;

personal friendships and loyalties may be cherished; but the group itself may be seen as an accidental result of religious or economic circumstances which no longer prevail. Education may lead to the decision to move out from the minority group. Nevertheless the examples surveyed do not always convince that what happens in schools determines the fate of a minority culture. It may well be that ultimately the deciding factor is not education in schools or universities but education in the family and neighbourhood and that this education has strength enough to ensure the survival of these group cultures.

4 The Mass Media and Minority Cultures

F. Y. St Leger

The study of the position of minority cultures in multicultural societies clearly involves an analysis not only at the specifically cultural level but at the socio-political one. Thus, the interaction of the cultural traits, values, beliefs, and tastes and of the institutionalised patterns of behaviour of two (or more) cultural groups takes place within, and is deeply affected by, the political ordering of the society in question, in particular by the political relationship between minority and majority groups. As well as the political structure, economic, social, demographic and other factors are relevant; it is the former, however, which is generally decisive.

The most important aspect of the political relationship between majority and minority—apart from that of the distribution of power between the two groups, which is almost always one of dominance by the majority—is, in Schermerhorn's terms, that of the centripetal or centrifugal approaches adopted by each group.[1] A centripetal approach seeks assimilation (at the cultural level, e.g. by destroying minority language(s) in favour of the majority one) or integration (on the socio-political one, e.g. by reducing or abolishing social segregation or by enfranchising the minority); a centrifugal one seeks to maintain separate cultural values, e.g. language, or religion, or to establish or maintain separate political institutions, such as those of 'home rule'. The extent to which majority and minority concur in either centripetal or centrifugal approach is vital. These 'approaches' or 'tendencies' may be partially implicit or unconscious; for example, it may be seen as 'natural' that Englishmen, i.e. members of the English body politic, should speak English, not Urdu or Polish, but ultimately such valuations tend to be embodied in political decisions, for example, in the recent decision by the inner London Education Authority with respect to the teaching of minority languages in schools.

The political, economic and socio-demographic variables are important as shaping the context in which the mass media operate, but their discussion in this chapter will be secondary to that of the role of the media themselves. Study of the mass media over the last half-century or so has resulted in an appreciable body of knowledge of its nature and effects, both in general and in relation to cultural change and social conflict, within as well as between societies. Sociological, socio-psychological and anthropological studies have also thrown much light on the results of interaction between cultures. It will be the aim of this chapter to apply what is known about mass communication to the current situation of cultural minorities, drawing as necessary on the political and other contextual elements.

Though clearly desirable, it will not be possible to construct a paradigm, let alone a theory, of mass communication and cultural minorities on a global scale. The argument will, however, be illustrated from time to time by specific examples. Finally, an attempt will be made to suggest social policy approaches to some of the problems of cultural minorities.

The mass media, for the purposes of this discussion, include radio and television, newspapers, magazines and books, the cinema, gramophone records and cassettes (audio and visual) but major attention will be given to television and the print media. In some contexts the differences between the media will require separate treatment; more often they will be discussed together.

CONTROL OF MASS MEDIA

Although Lasswell's well-known paradigm 'Who says What through Which Channel to Whom and with What Effects'[2] is now seen as too simplistic, especially in its implicit ignoring of the two-way relationship between the media and their environing society, it may still serve usefully to introduce the discussion. In the context of majority-minority relations we are concerned principally with the 'What' and 'Whom' and the 'Effects', more particularly with the cultural values carried by the media and received by members of the minority groups, and the ways in which their culture is modified as a result. In order to understand the content of the media message—the 'What'—it is however necessary to know something of those who control and effect the transmission of the messages.

The control of mass media output rests on a complicated balance between the owners, managers or formal controlling interests, such as newspaper proprietors or the State, on the one hand, and the staff of the newspaper or broadcasting organisation on the other. Such control has, of course, to take account of the demands and the pressures exerted by organisations and individuals in the environment, especially those of the audience. Research into the 'communicators' as opposed to the content or effects of mass communications has been relatively slight and much of it limited to the last 15 years; no body of reasonably firm findings comparable to those derived from research on effects has been established.

It would appear,[3] however, that:

1. The degree of control exercised over communicators differs between complete formal dependence, as in a broadcasting station run by a government department, to a formal independence, as on a newspaper such as *The Times* of London, where an editorial trust has been established safeguarding the latter's freedom. The actual degree of control exerted varies to an appreciable extent independently of the formal chain of command, and is expressed primarily through normative rather than utilitarian or coercive channels,[4] unwritten understandings and implicit cultural norms playing a major role.[5] One of the major issues in mass communication studies is the degree to which the media do serve as agencies for 'the engineering of consent' on behalf of dominant economic and political groups in society.[6] There is—perhaps unsurprisingly—relatively little hard evidence on this question. There is some evidence to suggest that the 'deep structure' or implicit values of media content reflects dominant societal values.[7]

2. Journalists are subject to a process of professional socialisation which is often more important than the overt organisational or political constraints upon them.[8] This professional ethos, which tends to be implicit rather than explicit, reflects the need to cater for the desires of a mass audience, the ethic of 'objectivity' and the partisan or social critic stance. The professional values of media

personnel are generally more important than their own idiosyncrasies or political views.

Journalistic values are subject to change and development, and to influence from the current cultural 'climate' of the environing society—the most obvious example is the growth of 'permissiveness' in the media but slightly more apt because less compatible with commercial criteria is the alleged 'leftward' emphasis in the electronic media in the late 1960s.[9]

CONTENT OF COMMUNICATIONS

The 'What', or content of mass communications has been much studied[10] but mainly either (1) as a reflection of the society in which they are produced[11] or of the characteristics, attitudes or purposes of the communicators or (2) in relation to effects. In either case content is, by definition, no more than a middle term. The principal exception to this statement is what may be called the problem of style, or rhetoric, not merely the objective, denotative or manifest meaning of the communication, but the overtones, the connotative or the latent meaning conveyed. The question of content is dealt with in concrete terms in relation to minority and majority cultures later in this chapter.

The relevance of the 'channels' is basically that they employ different 'media languages'.[12] The 'language' of film is quite different from that of print. The differences between these 'languages' is very relevant to the total meaning conveyed, hence potentially to the effects. The fact that different media to some extent reach or are used differently by different audiences, for example, the better educated tend to derive their information about the world predominantly from print rather than electronic media is calculated to emphasise the importance of these different 'languages'.

It is in relation to effects that most research has been done, hence that most reasonably confident generalisations can be made.

Berelson and Steiner provide a useful summary of the findings up to 1964.[13] For the present purpose the most important are:

1. The mass media serve to confirm attitudes already held rather than to induce change to new ones.

2. People tend to expose themselves to communications they expect to agree with their own views.

3. Material which is inconsistent with existing attitudes, opinions or beliefs tends to be either perceived selectively, i.e., those parts which disagree with one's attitudes are ignored, or are transmuted to fit one's preconceptions.

4. Communications on subjects on which no, or no strong attitude is held are more likely to be effective in shaping views than those in 1. above.

5. The mass media increase information on, or the salience of the issues they discuss; that is they 'set the agenda' or create images of the world.

6. Mass communication is mediated by, and functions in a matrix of face-to-face personal relations. There is a two- (or more-) step process in the adoption of ideological or material innovations, mediated and legitimised by opinion leaders, who tend to be more exposed to mass communications than their followers. In general, knowledge of a cultural innovation is derived from the mass media, but willingness to adopt it from inter-personal channels.

7. People who are in a marginal situation or exposed to cross-pressures are more likely than others to change their opinion as a result of mass communication.

8. In studies of 'modernisation' of underdeveloped societies the mass media are usually seen as an intervening rather than an independent variable:[14] they almost always function as part of a complex of variables, including urbanisation, literacy, empathy; the 'modern' culture traits are adopted, transmitted and legitimised by better educated, more cosmopolitan, higher social status individuals.

9. Mass media in a conflict situation tend to serve as a vehicle for a legitimating ideology for the in-group, which serves to cement it.[15]

In addition to these points on the mass media it is worth noting the following about culture change more generally:

1. Some elements of culture change more readily than others; thus technology, economic organisation, consumer life styles or recreational forms change more readily than language, religion or kinship structure. Broadly speaking, changes in the instrumental sphere are readily assimilated, less readily those in the cognitive sphere, least readily those in the sphere of values. In general, it is

the easily-assimilated elements, e.g. pop music, but also language and the values implicit in popular fiction, television dramas or advertisements that are most readily transmitted through the media.

2. Cultural change is not a simple one-way process; new culture elements may be transformed in the process of acceptance into a culture, alternatively they may elicit a reaction of 'back-lash', emphasising but often in the process changing some (opposing) feature of the original culture—common examples of both phenomena are found in the field of religion, e.g. the Cargo cults of Melanesia.

3. Parallelism and encapsulation are features of culture contact whereby logically contradictory ideas or even systems of conduct exist side by side in the same person, e.g. an African miner living (part of the time) on the Zambian copper belt may belong to a trade union and function as a worker as western *homo economicus*, but on his return to his village and farm may ignore economic in favour of social, ritual or even magical considerations.[16]

MINORITY–MAJORITY RELATIONS

It is now necessary to return to the question of minority–majority relations and to the role of the mass media in this context. The mass communicated messages originate (1) from the minority, (2) from the majority, or (3) from sources outside the society; the latter, of course, may operate direct, for example, through external radio broadcasts or imported books, or films, or indirectly through local translations or popularisations of foreign books or concepts. The balance between these three sources of media material will, of course, vary, depending on the size and wealth of the country concerned as a whole—the inhabitants of Lichtenstein or Nepal receive a relatively greater amount of foreign material than those of the United States or the Soviet Union—on the relative size, wealth and degree of sophistication of the majority and minority within that country, and on the political policies it pursues in relation to its minorities. In general, however, the majority will control a share of media outlets greater than the population ratios warrant.

This is true, firstly because of the high cost, in terms both of money and of expertise, of establishing and maintaining mass media outlets. Majorities are not only generally wealthier on a *per capita* basis, but *in toto* dispose of much greater resources than minorities. Insofar as governments are controlled by majorities (the usual case) and insofar as, partly for technical but much more for political reasons, radio and television are state or quasi-state monopolies, as again is true in nearly all countries outside North America the electronic media are more likely to be majority-controlled than the print media. The press in many countries is directly or indirectly government-controlled but even where it is not the cost of launching a new mass-circulation newspaper, for example, is only marginally less than that of establishing a broadcasting station and, in capitalist countries, adequate advertising support is essential for its survival. Particularly where minorities are relatively poor they may not form attractive targets for advertisers. Effective, mass-circulation minority newspapers are rare.[17] As between nations economic factors operate to produce media dominance by the wealthier societies. We shall return to this briefly in considering the content of media messages.

Not only is explicit political control or ownership of mass media outlets likely to be in majority hands but their personnel, especially professional or key personnel is likely to be recruited disproportionately from the majority groups. The under-representation of blacks on newspaper staffs and as film actors (except in very subordinate or stereotyped parts) in the United States, at least up to the 1960s is well documented,[18] and it seems probable that similar findings would emerge from a racial analysis of British television; as regards print journalism a writer in *New Community* estimates that of 28,000 journalists working on British newspapers or magazines only about two dozen are black.[19] It naturally follows that the media are likely to embody the attitudes and values and express the interest of the majority rather than the minority.

Similarly, access by minority groups to the media is usually limited in the sense that cultural material emanating from them, for example, music or drama seldom finds its way on to the television screens or into the newspapers or magazines controlled by the majority. The debate on 'access', not only for 'cultural minorities' in the sense the term is used in this book, but for any minority or sub-cultural group is currently a very live one in both Britain and the United States.

It should be noted that all the above factors, except those

embodying explicit political decisions may be completely unintentional results of the structure of society; hence the need for policies of positive discrimination. Control and staffing of the media are two of the factors responsible for media content. As, or more important, where market considerations apply—and by no means unimportant, even where the media are state-owned—are the attitudes, or the believed attitudes of readers, listeners or viewers. Failure to maintain or expand newspaper circulation sooner or later results in loss of advertising and ultimate bankruptcy. Similarly, loss of viewer ratings on commercial television will mean loss of advertising. A newspaper or television programme is a saleable product and must, therefore, within the limits of the alternatives open to it give the purchaser what he wants. Whether or not this means an appeal to a lowest common denominator of taste, as has so long been argued, it does imply a 'product' aimed at the majority.

It is surprisingly difficult to obtain a valid indication of what consumers want out of their newspapers or television programmes, or of what they could be persuaded to want. Neither the reporter, the features writer or script writer is able to produce material to a formula of audience reaction, nor indeed would this be regarded as their sole task.[20] Nevertheless, the journalist, whether in newspapers or in the electronic media does operate according to a set of mainly implicit assumptions relating to consumer reactions.[21] Thus, journalists share a common lore in relation to 'news values'—a lore which Galtung and Ruge, for example, have made explicit in their well-known study of foreign news in Norwegian newspapers.[22]

Two of the principles they enunciated were those of cultural 'distance' and of expectability. News which is neither about groups which are 'culturally close' to the readers/viewers nor conforms to the general expectations these have of the world will not readily be accepted. Minority groups, e.g., the Pakistanis in Britain are culturally 'distant' in this sense and the news deriving from them is likely to be in categories such as queer customs, violence, discrimination, etc.—news of Pakistani achievements in conventional fields would be less acceptable on the scale of news values. News media, in short, tend to accept and confirm their readers' stereotypes by the way they define news. The same is true, *mutatis mutandis*, in feature articles or films, and in fictional material.

Thus, several content analyses of American magazine fiction and of American films have shown that the WASP (White Anglo-Saxon Protestants) characters occupy the 'good' or major parts much more than their proportion in the population would justify.[23] Minority characters, where they appear at all, do so in minor, negative or socially subordinate, often stereotyped parts, such as the faithful retainer, or the 'clown'.

More generally, but also more subtly, mass media fictional content tends to embody a more or less idealised version of the dominant values of the society concerned, such as patriotism, individualism, achievement measured especially in economic or social class terms, the monogamous marriage based on romantic love and child-centred families.[24] The converse of this is the omission or negative portrayal of certain subjects such as divorce before the Second World War, certain social strata—manual workers are probably still much under-represented as heroes or heroines in popular fiction—or values.

There is a certain amount of evidence as to the extent and the ways in which minority cultures, in the United States, for example, share or differ from those of the majority,[25] but in general the mass media make rather little use of such material.[26] It is hardly necessary to add that where the majority culture is broadly consonant with the dominant values of international media content the pressure on minority values is that much greater and conversely—Christians in Lebanon or white (former) colonists in Kenya may feel their minority culture is immeasurably strengthened by its links with Christian, European or western culture.

The general statement of mass media production and content is refined and enriched when account is taken of the major contextual factors mentioned in the introduction to this chapter, specifically the political, economic, social and demographic variables, and the degree of difference between the cultures concerned, factors which, of course, are themselves interrelated. Most important is probably the political dimension. The first question to be asked about the political situation is whether majority and minority respectively are following a centripetal or centrifugal policy and how far the two groups agree on this policy.[27] Are the majority, for example, consciously pursuing a course of assimilation against the wishes of the minority? Or are the majority rejective of minority demands for assimilation, as in the case of Jews in pre-Second World War Germany or (though strictly a majority) Africans in South Africa. The distinction between cultural assimilation and social incorporation is a vital one; the two tend to be correlated, but by no means perfectly so. The latter point underlines the importance of the degree and nature of political power and rights enjoyed by the minority *vis-à-vis* the majority, both as individuals and as a group. The minority in Northern Ireland have (at least in principle) equal civil and political rights with the majority as individuals but not as a community, whereas the Dutch political system appears to confer both sorts of rights. Often more important than this question is the nature and degree of political organisation and the development of a political ideology among the minority; the political objectives and ideology of the minority interact closely with its cultural values, both as cause and effect. Nationalism is the affirmation of a social and political but also to a greater or lesser degree of a cultural identity; the cultural elements are usually more important in minority than in majority nationalism, where identification of the nation with the state gives it an explicitly political base. The relative poverty and inferior social status of the minority group tend to reinforce its motivation in political struggle against the majority, unless either this poverty breeds apathy or social class links take precedence over ethnic ones, as has, for example, been the aim of Soviet nationalities policy.

The relative size of majority and minority populations, and their degree of geographic segregation greatly affect the possibility of effective 'home rule', secession or even take-over of the state power. The degree of social segregation, which is correlated but by no means identical with geographic segregation is very relevant to the establishment of a common political identity, as well as to cultural differentiation. Conflict, as Coser has pointed out, involves the creation of legitimating ideologies and the establishment of cohesion within and on behalf of the conflicting groups.[28] The creation of cohesion relies upon the emphasising of common characteristics, including the social, economic and geographical ones mentioned above, but also the cultural ones, especially (as appropriate) language, religion and historical tradition. To these may be added literature, art, characteristic forms of recreation and particular life styles. The politicisation of majority-minority conflict ensures that the mobilisation of economic, social and cultural motivation is done consciously, on a comprehensive and organised basis.

The mass media commonly play an important role in such mobilisation, alongside such other agencies as political parties, trade unions, social or cultural and even welfare bodies. As has been mentioned where a minority does not control the state power it is normally excluded more or less from use of radio and television; the Dutch *verzuiling* system with minority access to radio and television production institutionalised in the political system is an exception. The main alternatives open to the minority are newspapers, magazines and book publishing, in that order of importance (except insofar as the publication of school books is concerned, that is, where the minority is able to control its own educational system).

Afrikaner nationalism in South Africa provides a good example of the co-ordination of political, religious, economic, educational and cultural organisations with the development of newspapers, magazines and book publishing.[29] It is noteworthy that Afrikaans newspapers initially had to be subsidised, in effect by the Nationalist Party; on the other hand the fact that two Nationalist Prime Ministers were former editors of Afrikaans newspapers is hardly fortuitous. After—and, though to a much lesser extent, before—1948, when the Nationalist Party finally took power, this minority was able to control radio, and when it was finally introduced in 1976, television broadcasting. The minority mass media in this instance undoubtedly fostered not only the political[30] but also the cultural values of Afrikanerdom, facilitating the upsurge of Afrikaans poetry and prose in the first third of the century, though the latter statement is more difficult to document.[31]

In a very different context the Dutch 'plural society' provides an interesting example of a society where the different blocs or 'pillars' (*Zuilingen*), Catholics (40 per cent), Dutch Reformed both *Herwormd* (28 per cent) and *Gereformeerd* (9 per cent) and those without religious affiliation (secular bloc, 18 per cent) combine a high degree of political, economic and social segregation with a fairly amicable *modus vivendi*.[32] These blocs also control not only different newspapers but each its own part of the broadcasting system—in fact any group which has at least 15,000 'paid-up' members can claim access, in terms of time, in proportion to its size.[33] The state, in short, acts not as the instrument of a dominant block, but to guarantee the rights of each of the religious minorities of which the population is composed, and underwrites—also by the subsidising of newspapers—the various minority mass media.

THE EFFECT ON MINORITIES

Given the control and content of mass communications and the context, political, economic and socio-demographic within which they operate, what effect do they have on the cultural minorities exposed to them? Correlatively what effect do they have on the majority's perception of the minority and on its cultural values? In some contexts this is a very important question. However, both for reasons of space and because an answer has been implied in what has already been said the response will be a laconic, if not cavalier one: the majority mass media predominantly reinforce either the ignorance or the negative stereotypes of the majority about the minority, and the minority media hardly penetrate to the majority (see figures of newspaper readership cited below). The effect of minority media on the minority insofar as it is culturally consonant—which, with the possible and partial exception of the values implicit in most advertising it is likely to be—will be to confirm the values and *Weltanschauungen* already held, hence preventing destruction of the culture by the majority. This, of course, is one example of the general effects of mass media noted above. The question of cultural invasion becomes acute only in relation to the impact of majority media on the minority.

Minorities may be protected from cultural 'invasion' in the first place by language and/or by illiteracy at least as far as concerns print media; if the latter they will, of course, be equally 'protected' from their own minority media. The same is true of the availability of mass media material, in technical, geographical and economic respects, e.g. a group living in a remote mountain area may be largely cut off from newspapers or, more generally, they may not be able to afford them. Television is probably not a potent threat to Kashmir or Transkei village culture, though the radio may be.

In considering the effect of the media on minorities it is necessary first to have some idea of how many of them attend to majority or minority communications respectively, what aspects of the material they attend to and thirdly how far their knowledge, attitudes or behaviour are influenced by these. In this connection the Afrikaner case will again be cited briefly. Table 4.1 summarises the relevant information.

Table 4.1 Readership of minority (Afrikaner) and majority (English) publications, 1968

in 000s	*Whites*			
	English speaking		*Afrikaans speaking*	
	No.	*% of group*	*No.*	*% of group*
Star (English daily)	327	33·2	140	10·1
Sunday Times (English weekly)	711	72·2	373	26·9
Vaderland (Afrikaans daily)	20	2·0	269	19·4
Beeld (Afrikaans weekly)	58	5·9	748	53·9

Source Market Research Africa, 1968. National Readership Survey, Johannesburg.

Note 'English-speaking' includes 'other'; 'Afrikaans-speaking' includes 'bilingual': both of these are small groups.

It is very clear that in this case, at least, majority readership of the minority press is negligible, but minority readership of the majority papers is very considerable. How far this relationship holds for minorities across the world would require further documentation but I would suggest that in very many cases—less so where the minority is large and is heavily concentrated in one region—the relationship would be found. It would certainly be true of American blacks,[34] or, probably, of other minority groups in the United States, probably of West Indians in Britain, and so on. That the majority do not read minority newspapers, magazines or books is more likely to be generally true than that minorities read an appreciable amount of majority newspaper output. How far minority media will enjoy the support of their own group will depend on various factors; several of these have already been mentioned, as applying to media generally, e.g. language, education, wealth and geographical factors, including the degree of dispersion or aggregation of the minority population. The degree of social segregation or of political discrimination/separation, particularly the former, is likely to have a powerful influence not only on the motivation to establish media outlets but on the willingness of minority members to read, listen to or view their own media output. The further removed the daily life, social and recreational, or religious activities of the minority member is from that of the majority the less likely is he to find any adequate reflection of this in the majority media. In the United States the gradual assimilation of immigrant groups has meant a great reduction in the immigrant press, which was very flourishing in the early part of this century, during and just after the great wave of migration from Europe.[35]

Because the electronic media are less often under minority control the question of competition between minority and majority media seldom arises; it may, however, be hypothesised that the same would be true as for the print media.

It is naturally more difficult to make any confident assertions about what aspects of the media are attended to by minority members or what effect the messages conveyed have on them than it is to say what newspapers they take or which broadcasting stations they tune in to. In general media use is more related to social class and to education than to ethnic or cultural identity. As indicated above, research shows that the better educated tend to prefer print rather than electronic media, and they tend to read or view more 'serious' material, e.g. political or economic analysis or quality literature or art, whereas the less well-educated and those of lower social status turn more to 'human interest', crime, sport, light comedy or thrillers. Insofar as the minority is generally poorer and less well-educated than the majority there will be some tendency for them to seek this sort of material in their media use. It also means that they will be more likely to use electronic rather than print media, hence majority rather than minority media.

Insofar as cultural change takes place first in the comparatively peripheral areas, as suggested above, it would seem likely that it is aspects of the media relating to such topics, generally sport and light entertainment, that will form the staple of minority reading or viewing and will have the most impact. The long opposition of Afrikaner Nationalist Governments in South Africa to the introduction of television was undoubtedly related, in part to their fear of cultural invasion by the 'English' and, perhaps permissive values conveyed by much imported television material.

Conversely, because, at least if the minority has been politicised, minority politics are salient for its members—they may, for example, have a range of political and economic grievances—the rank and file as well as the leaders, formal as well as opinion leaders will attend to and be influenced by the political content of minority mass communication, whereas political material in majority media will either not be attended to or will be rejected or re-interpreted through selective perception. Similarly, cultural material can be made salient to the reader/viewer as part of the minority *weltanschaung*, confirming his 'identity', as e.g. 'black' music or 'black' theology does for a black minority in a 'white' society.

The importance of advertising as a source of values frequently in conflict with those of the minority culture, especially where, as often, that culture is 'traditional', rural or ideologically conservative—as, for example, among the French Canadians, Afrikaner Calvinists,[36] or the Bretons in France—is clearly considerable. Insofar as its appeals are society-wide, and/or derived from an advertising 'sub-culture' based on the majority, or 'international' values—for example on monogamous, egalitarian marriage or fairly permissive patterns of child rearing—a subliminal appeal is made to (say) Pakistani families in Britain to conform to English or western values. Where advertisers are using minority media it is, of course, likely that advertisements will consciously be tailored more closely to the values of the recipients, but they may well still contain 'contrary messages' at a deep, often unconscious level.

SUMMARY

To summarise the argument of this chapter it is clear that the conditions of mass media production and diffusion as well as some of the insights of the sociological study of social change and of conflict do help considerably in understanding the role of mass communications in relation to minority cultures. First, the contextual factors which condition and modify the effect of the mass media are of vital importance. In particular the great importance of political organisation and ideology is clear. Secondly, the inbuilt and disproportionate dominance of the majority culture in terms of media ownership and/or content in the absence of vigorous attempts to 'redress the balance' is fairly well established. Thirdly, the impact of the mass media on minority cultures is likely, *ceteris paribus*, to be of fairly limited importance in comparison to factors such as education, involvement in the labour market and social integration, is likely to be greater in peripheral than in central cultural concerns (e.g. pop music rather than theology) and to operate more strongly where the majority culture is more complex than the minority one, e.g. the former is based on writing where the latter is not. In general, however, the evidence on effects—particularly the long-term effects which are of interest in this context—is much weaker than that for the first two conclusions, and is largely inferential or circumstantial in nature.

Given the basic assumption that (a) cultural diversity, in terms of ethnic as well as other values or life-ways enriches the whole of society and/or (b) that the cultural heritage of a group is to be included among the goods, if not the rights which a government should seek to facilitate for the members of that group insofar as this is consonant with overall social justice, there are nevertheless so many factors peculiar to a given situation that any statement of policy implications must be very cautious. If, however, it is desired to cherish the contribution of a specific minority culture it would seem that first, a vigorous policy of 'positive discrimination' needs to be followed. A useful analogy here is such a policy in relation to socially-deprived areas of British or American cities—which are, in fact, often inhabited disproportionately by ethnic minorities—or in ethnic 'quotas' in American colleges. This could be done through greater employment of the minority members in broadcasting, by increasing the number of hours allocated to broadcasts in the minority language or devoted to minority features or by the establishment of a separate channel or broadcasting station, the latter particularly appropriate where the minority is concentrated in one part of the country. Radio or television forums, where any group which wishes may use a time 'slot' to put on its own production is a method recently brought into use in Britain, and institutionalised under the Dutch system.

'Access' in these terms is, however, probably of rather limited effectiveness, a 'slot' on 'someone else's media' being less useful than full control of one's own.

Second, political organisation of the minority, coupled, as it often is with the control of its own mass media needs to be facilitated. The means whereby the former may be done are the staple of much of the political debate in 'plural societies' —devices such as 'home rule', proportional representation, communal franchises, 'power-sharing' in one shape or another are well known, though variously effective; the Dutch 'pillar' (*zuiling*) system seems to be one of the most successful but is not necessarily exportable. In the present context the main emphasis must fall on direct government encouragement of minority media. This might involve, for example, state subsidies (as in the Netherlands and some other countries) to minority as well as majority newspapers. Of course, this presupposes a political culture of unusual tolerance and fairness. Clearly, control by a minority of its own education system is calculated to buttress the role of the minority media while economic advance would make it more feasible both because it would provide the money for the establishment of minority media and because it would enable more minority members to consume the products of these media.

Thirdly, in relation to minority cultures which are not offshoots linked to a major international culture the curtailment of foreign material on the nation's airwaves may indirectly benefit the more vulnerable minority culture more than the majority, though in many of the smaller countries, at least, both may be 'at risk', and if the foreign material is replaced by greater emphasis on majority productions, as e.g. in Malaysia the minority, in that case both the Chinese and the Indians, may even be worse off.[37]

All the above suggestions refer to policies which might be pursued by democratic governments with a commitment to the encouragement of cultural diversity within a common unitary or federal political system. The policy implications for the leadership of minority groups are fairly obvious correlates of these. Their task, for example, is not only to endeavour to establish new media outlets but to imbue those that do exist with a sense both of the minority's identity and of its cohesion, its common interests and values.

This brief discussion has been in the nature of a reconnaissance in force rather than an attack on its subject. Hopefully, however, it has served to identify points where more intensive pressure may be applied, and the beginnings at least of a theoretical schema constructed.

NOTES

1. R. A. Schermerhorn, *Comparative Ethnic Relations* (New York, 1970), p. 81.

2. H. D. Lasswell, 'The Structure and Function of Communication in Society' in L. Bryson, *The Communication of Ideas* (New York, 1948).
3. J. Tunstall, *Media Sociology* (London 1970); *Journalists at Work* (London 1971); and D. McQuail, *Towards a Sociology of Mass Communication* (London 1970).
4. A. Etzioni, *Complex Organisations* (Glencoe, 1961).
5. W. Breed, 'Social Control in the Newsroom', *Social Forces,* vol. 33, no. 1 (1955), pp. 326–35; J. Tunstall, *op. cit.* (1970); T. Burns, 'The Public Service and Private World', *Sociological Review Monograph,* no. 13 (1969), pp. 53–73; and P. Elliott, *The Making of a Television Series* (London, 1972).
6. H. Marcuse, *One-dimensional Man* (London, 1964); C. W. Mills, *The Power Elite* (New York, 1956); R. Williams, *Communications* (Harmondsworth, 1966).
7. Glasgow University Media Research Group, *Bad News* (1976); S. Hall, 'The Determination of News Photographs', *Working Papers in Cultural Studies, no. 3*; also his 'Broadcasting, Politics and the State: the Independence/Impartiality Conflict', unpublished paper delivered to the International Association for Mass Communications Research Conference, Leicester, 1976; A. C. H. Smith, *Paper Voices: the Popular Press and Social Change 1935–1965* (London, 1973).
8. W. Breed, *op. cit.* (1955); J. Tunstall, *op. cit.* (1970); and R. W. Stark, 'Policy and the Pro's: an Organizational Analysis of a Metropolitan Newspaper', *Berkeley Journal of Sociology* (1963), pp. 11–31.
9. A. Smith, *The Shadow in the Cave* (London, 1973).
10. B. Berelson, *Content Analysis in Communication Research* (Glencoe, 1952); O. Holsti, *Content Analysis for the Social Sciences and the Humanities* (Reading, 1969).
11. D. C. McClelland, *The Achieving Society* (New York, 1961) and D. Reissman *et al.*, *The Lonely Crowd* (New Haven, 1950).
12. A. Tudor, 'Film, Communication and Content' in J. Tunstall, *op. cit.* (1970); M. McLuhan, *Understanding Media* (London, 1964).
13. B. Berelson and G. A. Steiner, *Human Behaviour, an Inventory of Scientific Findings* (New York, 1964).
14. D. Lerner, *The Passing of Traditional Society* (New York, 1958); L. Pye, *Communications and Political Development* (Princeton, 1963) and E. M. Rogers and F. F. Shoemaker, *The Diffusion of Innovations* (New York, 1971).
15. L. A. Coser, *The Functions of Social Conflict* (Glencoe, 1956).
16. C. Mitchell, *Social Networks in Urban Situations* (Manchester, 1971) and P. Mayer, *Townsmen or Tribesmen* (London, 1971).
17. It is not possible, nor perhaps necessary, fully to document this generalisation here, but the following examples may be given. In the United States the black (Negro) population numbers about 18 million or about 9 per cent of the total but it controls only 3 of 1756 daily English-language newspapers. R. E. Wolseley, *The Black Press* (Iowa, 1971).
18. C. Hartman and C. Husband, *Racism and the Mass Media* (New York, 1974).
19. L. Morrison, 'A Black Journalist's Experience of British Journalism', *New Community,* vol. IV, no. 3, pp. 317–22.
20. T. Burns (1969), *op. cit.*

21. I. Shulman and I. Pool, 'Newsmen's Fantasies, Audiences and Newswriting' in L. A. Dexter and D. M. White, *People, Society and Mass Communications* (Glencoe, 1964).
22. J. Galtung and M. H. Ruge, 'The Structure of Foreign News', in J. Tunstall, *op. cit.* (1970), pp. 259–300.
23. M. U. Martel and G. J. McCall, 'Reality-Orientation and the Pleasure Principle', in L. A. Dexter and D. M. White, *op. cit.* (1964); B. Berelson and P. J. Salter, 'Majority and Minority Americans: an Analysis of Magazine Fiction', *Public Opinion Quarterly*, vol. 10, no. 2 (1946); C. Hartman and C. Husband, *op. cit.* (1974), Chapter 9.
24. S. W. Head, 'Content Analysis of Television Drama Programmes', *Quarterly of Film, Radio, and Television*, vol. 9 (1954), pp. 175–94; D. V. McGranahan and I. Wayne, 'German and American Traits Reflected in Popular Drama', *Human Relations*, vol. 1, no. 4 (1948), pp. 429–55; D. Reissman *et al.*, *op. cit.* (1950); D. C. McClelland, *op. cit.* (1961).
25. St. Clair Drake and H. R. Cayton, *Black Metropolis* (New York, 1945); G. Myrdal, *An American Dilemma* (New York, 1944); J. Dollard, *Caste and Class in a Southern Town* (New York, 1949); F. Frazier, *The Negro in the United States* (London, 1957); F. Kluckhohn and F. L. Strodtbech, *Variations in Value Orientations* (Evanston, 1961).
26. Kerner Commission, *Report of the National Advisory Commission on Civil Disorders* (New York, 1968); P. Elliott, *op. cit.* (1972).
27. R. A. Schermerhorn, *op. cit.* (1970), p. 83.
28. L. A. Coser, *op. cit.* (1956) and *Continuities in the Study of Social Conflict* (Glencoe, 1967).
29. L. Thompson and M. Wilson, *The Oxford History of South Africa* (Oxford, vol. II, 1971).
30. R. Ainslie, *The Press in Africa* (London, 1966), Chapters 3, 5; E. Potter, *The Press as Opposition* (London, 1975).
31. E. S. Munger, *Afrikaner and African Nationalism* (London, 1967), p. 48 footnote.
32. C. Bagley, *The Dutch Plural Society* (London, 1973), J. Goudsblom, *Dutch Society* (New York, 1967).
33. A. Smith, *op. cit.* (1973).
34. R. E. Wolseley, *op. cit.* (1971).
35. R. Park, *The Immigrant Press and its Control* (New York, 1922), R. E. Wolseley, *op. cit.* (1971), p. 323.
36. W. A. De Klerk, *The Puritans in Africa* (London, 1975).
37. R. Adhikasya, *Broadcasting in Peninsular Malaysia* (London, 1976).

5 Economic Support for Minority Languages

Terence O'Brien

To grow
a second tongue, as
harsh a humiliation
as twice to be born.

Decades later
that child's grandchild's
speech stumbles over lost
syllables of an old order.

The poet John Montague explored the effects on a community when a subordinate linguistic culture collapsed under pressures from a more dominant culture.[1] This discussion concentrates on language because it has been held to constitute the essence of a culture. George Steiner put the point this way:

> Language is both the container and the shaping spirit of the ways in which we experience the world. Every single language embodies and gives expression to a particular way of organising perceiving, understanding reality. Human senses are, broadly speaking, the same throughout the earth. But the mental picture of the world which makes up that complex living framework of social existence which we call a culture varies immensely from community to community. And it is of this variety that language is the pre-eminent medium and preserver.[2]

Is it the economic interest of man that thousands of minority languages be preserved? Was not Babel rightly perceived by the ancients as a disaster for mankind? Multiplicity of languages are an obstacle to trade and the mobility of labour, technology and information generally. In the multicultural state with neither tariff nor border checks to hinder trade or labour mobility language can constitute a major barrier to economic integration and the increase in living standards assumed to accompany that process. In certain African states today the multiplicity of languages slows modernisation by impeding the dissemination of fundamental knowledge important to human wellbeing such as hygiene and agricultural techniques.

Emphatically this does not mean that very small linguistic communities must inevitably suffer from relative backwardness which develops into decline and extinction. Given certain prerequisites, such as a measure of control over the disposal of the surplus generated from local resources, such communities can remain vigorous. The example of the Icelanders and the Faroe islanders demonstrates that communities with minute populations can survive and develop a technologically modern society which operates effectively through the medium of a distinctive minority language, despite the debilitating influence of long-term net outward migration.[3] Are there many other small linguistic communities with the potential to imitate Faroese example?

The works of Stephens, Petrella, Steiner and others show minority languages to be under pressure in western Europe and throughout the world. Points of current debate are first, should there be intervention to arrest this decline? And secondly, if it is accepted that action should be taken, what form should it take?

When a community places a high value on its language it could be held that the welfare of its members was diminished by the erosion of that language. But how can the value which a community attaches to its language be assessed objectively? One measurement might be the willingness of the community individually and collectively to pay in order to preserve its language. Preparedness to pay may take one of the following forms:

1. income and occupational opportunities forgone by staying at home rather than migrating to economically more attractive locations outside the language area;

2. organisation and agitation to bring about administrative and other changes favourable to the language;

3. a determination in the face of disabilities and handicaps to

speak the language and pass it on to the next generation.

Is the matter not then best left to the interaction between individual and communal values and economic and cultural forces? Communities prepared to pay the price will preserve their linguistic cultural identities and those which do not place a sufficiently high valuation on their heritage will lose it. Admittedly, geographical and other influences will cause the costs of preserving linguistic identity to vary significantly as between one minority and another but are not such disparities a feature of all aspects of life which have to be accepted?

The reality is that languages are now dying at an alarming rate and this process will presumably continue. There is a sadness about the passing of any well established aspect of a culture, which can be heard in the bardic laments for the old Gaelic social order or the heart's cry by William Blake against the destruction of the craftsman. Blake held that mechanisation diminished workers as human beings and so also the communities in which they interacted socially. Steiner argues in a parallel way that the destruction of minority languages diminishes mankind.

> As more and more of the tongues of men flicker into oblivion, or into the cold ash of the ethnographer's filing-cabinet, the richness and the potential of human spontaneity of the re-inventions of life and purpose on this wasted planet, diminish also. Each and every human tongue is a distinct window on to the world. Looking through it, the native speaker enters an emotional and spiritual space, a framework of memory, a promontory on tomorrow, which no other window in the great house at Babel quite matches. Thus, every language mirrors and generates a possible world, an alternative reality.
>
> This, I believe, is the clue or the riddle we began with. The seemingly absurd, economically crippling, socially and politically divisive multiplicity of human tongues—a multiplicity going into the thousands—represents an absolutely essential mechanism of human freedom. Because each language constitutes a different part of the total range of possible consciousness and personal identity, men have been free to dream, to invent, to analyse in a multitude of different ways.[4]

If Steiner's argument is accepted then the death of a minority language represents a loss both to the community immediately concerned and to the world community but more particularly to the state or federation of which that minority culture is a part. It would follow that the wider state should, in equity, be prepared to bear part of the costs necessary to halt the decline of a minority language, in a proportion related to an estimate of the gains derived by the wider community. But there is no way of assessing, in any objective sense, the actual or potential benefits which Steiner attributes to the existence of minority languages. Hence decisions as to the degree of support which a wider community will make available to assist the fortunes of a minority language will not be guided by a rational calculation of costs as against expected benefits but will be determined solely by political and financial pressures and constraints. For the committed supporter of a minority language under pressure the task would therefore appear to be one of maximising political support while minimising demands for financial aid.

THE ECONOMICS OF HALTING LINGUISTIC DECLINE

Moving from the general to the particular, the foregoing arguments can be applied to the European Economic Community and the position of peripheral linguistic minorities in what is developing into one of the world's larger multicultural states.[5]

Excluded from consideration in this short chapter are dialects and minorities speaking major European languages. Examples of the latter are the German speaking Belgians and the French, Serbo-Croat and German speaking minorities in Italy, which essentially represent a set of border rather than peripheral problems. However, references are made to the German-Italian question because it is well documented. Also excluded are minority language groups such as speak Arabic, Urdu and Hindi which were formed by immigration from ex-colonies, or by migrant workers from within and without the Community such as Turks, Greeks, Spaniards, Portuguese or Italians. Their needs do not merit less attention than those of minority language groups in peripheral areas but their situation differs in two respects. They are largely settled in urban centres in developed areas and they are all branches of well established linguistic cultures.

Turning then to the periphery let us assume that the peoples of Europe are persuaded of the merits of maintaining the vitality of the minority linguistic cultures and that this view has been transmitted to the governing organs of the new Europe; Parliament, Commission and Ministerial Council. Assume again that there is agreement in principle to take supportive action, three questions would then arise, namely:

1. What are the objectives?

2. What is the range of options open whereby those objectives might be attained?

3. What is the cost of attaining the specified objectives by operating through the options?

Objectives

Accept that the minimal objective is to slow the rate of decline in peripheral minority languages within the shortest possible time and that the maximum objective is to halt the decline.

Options

It is for the sociolinguist to identify and weight the influences causing the decline of a particular language and to specify the range of measures that will halt or reverse decay. These measures may be classified according to the speed with which they can be expected to counteract the process of decline. Such diagnoses must necessarily differ as between one case and another such as Breton and Frisian, and the prognoses also. Given the minimal objective specified, attention would be concentrated on those measures which have an impact in the short term i.e. from 1 to 3 years. These can be crudely categorised thus:

(a) to reduce outward migration by stimulating economic activity;

(b) to strengthen a language by means of administrative or institutional changes such as by promoting greater use by the local bureaucracy or the educational system;

(c) to promote a language by means of media provision e.g. television, radio, films, records, cassettes, newspapers, periodicals, books.

Cost of attaining specified objectives

To use the jargon we now come to the interface between economics and applied linguistics. It is the economist's task to rank an array of measures according to their estimated cost in relation to their expected effectiveness. With guidance, the economist can arrive at cost estimates but he is entirely in the hands of the linguist when it comes to establishing measures of effectiveness. This exercise is necessary for the economist because he is called on to carry out one of the following tasks:

given a stated objective, specify the measures which may be taken to attain it using a minimum of financial resources; or

given a limited allocation of resources, specify the measures which will result in the greatest advance towards a stated objective.

In either case he is concerned to establish relationships between cost and effectiveness and it is in this area that economists and linguists have a fruitful area for co-operation.

CONCRETE SITUATIONS

Economic forces are speeding the decay of minority languages in peripheral areas of the European Community.[6] The characteristics of most of these areas show, in exaggerated form, the low incomes and socio-economic under-development of the regions of which they form a part. Practically all peripheral areas have high rates of net emigration.

A high proportion of employment is in traditional resource-based industries such as agriculture and fishing and the local economy cannot absorb those seeking work in alternative occupations. The peripheral problem is the regional problem writ large. Not all peripheral regions are coincident with linguistic minorities but the relationship is significant because it is not accidental that minority languages in the EEC are found at the periphery, on islands, promontories and in barren and mountainous terrain. Their very survival has been partly a function of a remoteness which reduced contacts with the dominant language. Remoteness, which in the past was a protection for the culture, today puts the societies at an economic disadvantage which is adversly affecting their languages. The case for assistance to these economies seems straightforward.

> The protection of minorities is not merely a legal and cultural phenomenon: just as important, if not more so, it is an economic and social question, since economic power provides the where-

withal of a minority to exist and social flexibility is vital if a minority is to remain on competitive terms with the majority in a world of swift technological progress.[7]

But the issue is not so straightforward. It is difficult to make a strong case for special aid for the economies of areas with linguistic minorities, on the sole basis of the linguistic uniqueness of their cultures because an attempt to do them justice may result in an injustice to other groups. Should communities at the tip of Jutland or the toe of Italy have less support in dealing with their economic situation than Corsicans or Basques? Should Orcadians merit a lower level of assistance to cope with emigration than Hebrideans because the former do not speak a minority language? The issue was raised in 1977 in Ireland. West coast islanders claimed they suffered discrimination in the matter of state aids because they were English-speakers although their economic and social position was, in every particular, similar to that of their more favourably treated neighbours on Gaelic speaking islands.

This grievance is happily being remedied, but the lesson is clear. If the search is for a set of general principles to guide a joint European policy favourable to linguistic minorities, then to urge discriminatory aid to benefit the economies of these areas as a means of cultural support would be unwise. A more soundly based approach would be to press for an adaptation of present regional policy so that it discriminated more acutely in favour of all areas sharing characteristics of severest social and economic deprivation which would automatically include those areas inhabited by most of the peripheral linguistic minorities without penalising areas which are similarly disadvantaged but lack linguistic uniqueness.

Minority language groups do have a claim to exclusive financial aid arising from the pressures being currently experienced. But, as is argued elsewhere, such claims to exclusivity must be demonstrably linked to support for the language. Thus demands for school texts or mass media provision in the vernacular cannot be duplicated by groups other than linguistic minorities whereas demands for assistance via such an indirect intermediary as the economy can be.

There is an extensive literature on regional economics and the problems of the west European regions in particular. One remarkable feature is that, with the exception of the 'Galway Declaration' (see below) on a general intellectual level the debate on the situation of the European regions is taking place without reference to the linguistic/cultural dimensions of the economic problems besetting the periphery. The idea that financial aid to the regions might be required for other than economic objectives is rarely explored. Yet strong arguments can be put forward to support such aid. It could help to remove some of the tensions which are currently in evidence in a number of EEC member states between language minorities and national governments.

Regional Policy

There is no shortage of analyses and suggested policies to narrow the imbalance in incomes as between the regions and the centrally developed areas of the Community. Lacking is the political will to co-ordinate and fund a comprehensive policy. At the Galway meeting attended by representatives from half of the sixty peripheral regions and countries of the Council of Europe trenchant criticisms of the European Community's concept of regional policy were made which were summarised thus:

> The consequences of this situation are manifold and are above all of extreme gravity: injustice, social inequality and emigration; high costs, wasted resources and inflation; process of colonisation of peripheral regions by central regions and finally centrifugal forces in relation to European unification.[8]

In what is now known as the 'Galway Declaration' delegates called for 'a massive European programme of infrastructural work concerning the communication network for peripheral Europe'. This was considered important because 'it is clear that it is the insufficiency of the European transport and communication system which hinders the peripheral areas of Europe from benefiting from the industrialisation and from the agricultural progress necessary to put an end to emigration or to reduce the numbers of underemployed and unemployed'.

This is a prescription which would tend to work in the medium- rather than the short-term. Nor does it take account of the special transport problems facing peripheral communities separated from the European mainland by water, such as Greenland, the islands off the Scottish and Irish coasts (which are doubly removed) and the Corsicans, Sards, Sicilians and Frisians. In logic the argument would seem to imply transport subsidies for island regions. However, the economic side effects of current cost transport subsidies are immensely complex and the short run effects might even increase local unemployment in certain peripheral areas.

The Ultimate Periphery

The Galway conference included representatives from Hamburg and other parts of Europe which are peripheral in geographical terms but not in the sense of being economically marginal. To avoid ambiguity areas both remote and economically underdeveloped are here termed 'the ultimate periphery'. The Scottish Highlands constitutes a prime example of such an area. Prattis, referring to the Highlands, said:

> policies designed to develop the marginal regions based on the strategy of increased exposure to modern market forces misunderstand that the existing marginality itself is a result of exposure to modern market forces. Furthermore such policies will serve only to increase the relative marginality of the economically backward regions. In other words development policy is useless unless it is designed to alter the structure of relationships between the marginal region and the modern sector. If there is to be a realistic solution to marginality then it should be realised that development only follows upon changes in the structure of interdependence that link the market economy with its marginal sectors. Furthermore the extent of restructuring is an important evaluative criterion in assessing whether policies to eradicate marginality have in fact been successful . . .
>
> The marginal economy does not have the opportunity to diversify and with increasing control of its economy by entrepreneurs and agencies located in the progressive modern sector it then becomes the source for primary and extractive products that the modern sector manufactures and distributes. The marginal sector is used instrumentally by the modern sector and indeed becomes functional to the maintenance of the continual growth of the modern sector.[9]

According to Prattis, lack of diversification is associated with past failure to develop new opportunities by reinvesting part of the economic surplus. From his thesis it can be inferred that a crucial step in altering the nature of the relationship with the developed sector is to create an economic mechanism that will net part of the surplus and reinvest it for the benefit of the people in the area. The development of such a mechanism does not necessarily imply formal political devolution.

Economic Development

Meic Stephens has cited numerous examples from West Friesland to Sardinia, where the minority language has been damaged by the process of economic modernisation.[10] This modernisation is itself inevitable and ultimately necessary but must it always injure the minority language? If economic development can damage the vernacular in large minority communities how much more vulnerable are those where the minority language speakers are numbered in thousands rather than tens or hundreds of thousands? The establishment of enterprises from outside a community may also lead to a situation where a high proportion of occupations commanding power and respect are held by incoming monoglots from the majority culture, which further weakens the social position of the minority language. The smaller the minority, the less likely it is to have manpower trained in new technologies, and unless special arrangements are made to train minority speakers for such posts the incoming industry will import them from outside. In a chemical industry, for example, it is the unskilled and semi-skilled posts that would tend to go to the indigenous minority speakers and the community would have imported an economic organisation the social influence of which might help to undermine the linguistic basis of its culture.

As recently as August 1977, a co-operative in a *Gaeltacht* (Gaelic-speaking area) in the west of Ireland, issued a statement drawing attention to the way in which industrial grants, designed to strengthen the economic base of the district, were in practice being made use of in a way which eroded the language.

> The trends that we speak about concern the transfer of Galway-based industries to nearby Gaeltacht factories in Connemara. The only reason for such transfers appears to be to avail of the

> higher Gaeltacht industrial grants and not out of any love or loyalty to the Gaeltacht . . .
> The same industries, while giving an undertaking to employ local labour, are, in fact, employing their former English-speaking employees from Galway and transporting them in and out of the areas on a daily basis . . .
> We see in this trend another important factor in the gradual decay of the Gaeltacht areas in this country. Our concern has already been personally conveyed to the new Minister for the Gaeltacht in this regard.[11]

Economic development is not therefore the cure-all solution to the difficulties presently being experienced by minority languages. An increase in the rate of economic development can, as illustrated above, serve to advance the dominant language unless the process is supervised. Broadly speaking, the weaker the language the less can its guardians permit economic development to be initiated from outside especially when the introduction of high level technological industries are concerned. Where the agencies with responsibility for economic development are controlled by central government a policy of inducing outside enterprise to establish in the peripheral areas is frequently adopted, in preference to the more difficult alternative of helping the indigenes to initiate development themselves.

The latter approach has been encouraged with some success in the Gaelic speaking areas of the west of Ireland where agricultural producer and marketing co-operatives are beginning to take root and expand. These serve to nurture local commercial leadership and increase communal self confidence. The co-operative approach to organisation has spread to the provision of tourist facilities and public utilities. The natural line of development for such resource-based co-operative enterprises is to create added value by engaging in successively more sophisticated stages of marketing and/or processing. Nor is this generalisation based on Irish experience. Indeed more apposite examples can be quoted from Wales, Brittany or South Tyrol.

A recent example of the co-operative approach to development being adopted as official policy comes with the announcement in November 1977, by the Chairman of the Highlands and Islands Development Board, that money and staff are being made available to the Gaelic-speaking areas to promote this type of organisation:

> It is a long-term programme which, if proved worthwhile, could strengthen the Islands' social and economic fabric. What we are talking about is a type of co-operation that has not been tried in Scotland before. These organisations, which are operating in Ireland, are not confined to one activity. They can run hotels, knitwear factories, market gardens, provide services, organise social facilities—the possible combinations are endless.[12]

In reality, support for co-operatives is likely to be but one strand in any official strategy to strengthen the economies of the ultimate periphery. While not idealising or overemphasising the value of co-operative economic organisation its potential contribution must be fully appreciated. Co-operative organisation represents a mechanism which can gather and reinvest the economic surplus generated locally for local benefit. It is an instrument which can, without changes in the formal political structure, change the relationships between the ultimate periphery and the modern sector. Furthermore, what is sometimes overlooked is that the co-operative enterprise, in its formative stages, very frequently produces joint products; goods or services as well as psychological benefits and it is the latter which may be of greatest value to minority cultures under pressure. It can turn despair into hope and any system which can accomplish that has a value on a par with the good wife; beyond price.

It is also necessary to answer doubts often expressed as to the ability of co-operative type organisations to provide significant industrial employment in manufacturing activities other than processing. The experience of the engineering co-operatives in Mondragon[13] in the Basque region of Spain give grounds for optimism but whether this successful experiment can be replicated in other areas is still an open question.

When therefore, economic measures are being considered as a means of bringing *swift* assistance to minority languages under pressure two points need to be borne in mind.

(i) The relationship between the fortunes of minority languages and the effects of economic policies is as yet imperfectly understood. The economist and the linguist need urgently to examine economic developments in the minority language areas to identify those developments which tend to weaken or strengthen the local language.

(ii) The economies of the 'ultimate periphery' will remain marginal until there is a means of diversifying the economies.

ADMINISTRATIVE/INSTITUTIONAL CHANGES

It could be argued that the weaker a minority linguistic culture the greater the control that community must be able to exercise over its economic and social life if it is to survive. Unfortunately, today in Europe minority cultures with adequate local autonomy are the exception. Historical tensions between the centre and the regions led in the past to the repression of minority languages and in some EEC countries time has not allayed centralist suspicions and consequently the economic weakness of some minority cultures is compounded by the existing local administrative structures. These difficulties extend from economic affairs to the linguistic implications of education policy and media provision.

The recognition of this situation almost invariably leads to demands by the minorities for a form of local autonomy. But, as Stephens illustrates, with reference to Sardinia, unless linked into a strong local movement concerned to deal with economic and cultural problems, devolution will not of itself guarantee the revival of a declining language.[14]

COMMUNICATIONS

It is to media provision, with particular reference to radio and television that discussion now turns. Unless the effectiveness of a particular measure is demonstrably superior to rival or alternative approaches a strategy designed to halt language atrophy is unlikely to place total reliance on any one instrument, such as employment creation, to the exclusion of possibilities offered by institutional changes or communications. For the economist looking for returns in the short run the task is to apportion resources among the available instruments so as to achieve the right balance in terms of outlay and effectiveness. Given, for example, an annual subvention of £1 million to support Sard, should that money be spent to expand rural co-operatives, provide teaching materials for schools or extend local broadcasting; or how should the allocation be divided as between these? The fact is that in the absence of objective measures of short-run effectiveness it is necessary to fall back on a variety of arguments in order to establish priorities. If one is looking for the greatest returns in the short run the case for giving priority to investment in media provision seems strong. When investment is in new employment provision the short-term effect is for the major benefits to go to the few. When investment is in the education system the returns mature in the medium- and long-term. But with investments in radio and television broadcasting the benefits are fairly immediate and are available to the many. There are also well established methodologies to monitor audience response and hence to test some aspects of effectiveness.

Both Petrella and Stephens documented the amount of broadcasting time given to linguistic minorities and with the exception of Irish and Welsh the provision made by national governments in the EEC is either inadequate or non-existent. In this situation the returns to a modest provision of radio and television time could be very high.

Access to adequate broadcasting time is therefore a platform on which all the minorities can find common ground. This issue is especially important to those linguistic minorities which cannot benefit from access to broadcasts from a kin-state. German-speaking Italians can avail of transmissions from four states to the north but Corsicans can draw on no such external support.

It could be argued in opposition that in giving Breton only a few hours radio time a week there is no injustice because on the basis of numbers and the broadcasting time available this is all that the Bretons are entitled to. But this argument misses the essential point at issue.

> . . . for the protection of minorities one needed equality, but this equality must be more than formal, it had to be effective, and this meant that the minority should have the facility and possibility of satisfying its own interests, and spiritual, cultural, economic, administrative, and political needs with means as effective as those used by the majority. There was no greater inequality than to treat equally unequal things. Therefore special laws to protect a minority were not privileges but measures to create this material equality between majority and minority.[15]

In the Tyrolese dispute the Italian Government claimed that the minority had full equality of rights. Alcock comments:

> Unfortunately, equality of rights is not suitable for dealing with minorities who, for one reason or another, are in a state of inferior economic and social development compared to the majority and who, unsurprisingly, seek not only equality in this development but means to enable this equality to be an on-going process.[16]

In terms of the speed with which it can be inaugurated, the numbers upon whom it will impinge and the cost of provision, investment in media services would seem to have first priority given a policy of short-term action to halt the decline in a language. In the socio-chemical process whereby a community under cultural attack breeds antibodies to fight off the threat to its language a local radio-television facility can, in an indirect way, stimulate the forces of resistance. Thus self-help and co-operative economic endeavours are quickly communicated and beget imitators while dissatisfaction with administrative practices are given a point of focus. This is of crucial importance where there are no daily newspapers in the minority languages, and the communities are scattered geographically.

No attempt is made here to elaborate on the economics of media provision. Suffice it to say that the average current cost of an initial or additional hour in radio time in a minority language is moderate. The problem arises where limitation of channels means that an hour allocated to a minority language results in the loss of an established broadcasting time to the dominant language. Consequently a serious attempt to make available more than token provision usually implies the establishment of a local station with the capital outlay that involves. But when it is realised that many linguistic minorities are not at present conceded even token provision, and that such could be supplied at minimal cost, it will be understood that political attitudes towards the nature of the state and not shortage of funds are the real obstacle to such provision.

Euradio is an agency of the European Commission which supplies material relative to the work of the Community to the media in the member states. By arrangement with the European Broadcasting Union it may be possible to expand its role so as to give greater support to minority language broadcasting agencies.

THE POLITICAL DIMENSION

Mention was made earlier of minimising financial demands and maximising political pressures. Before 1980 the first directly elected European Parliament is due to assemble at Strasbourg. This institution will provide minority language areas with a forum in which they can present their grievances to the whole of Europe. Whether this can be an effective means of putting pressure on national governments depends to a large extent on the ability of the minorities to organise and to set themselves realistic objectives. If minority language groups desire European policies which take their needs into consideration it will be necessary to have an active lobby at work. Already the European socialists have come together to draw up commission policy positions and these at present do not take cognisance of the special needs of minority language areas. There are grounds for hope. The Bureau of Unrepresented Nationalities has established an office in Brussels[17] and in co-ordination with the Belgian *Volksunie*, the Celtic League,[18] and European members of parliament sympathetic to linguistic minorities there is the possibility of developing a lively pressure group.

It is interesting to note that in the case of the border minorities, the existence of an external power interested in their welfare has not been without influence. The German-speaking Belgian minority is treated with every consideration. The classic case is the German-speaking minority in Italy. The existence of external pressures from Vienna and elsewhere helped to bring about an equitable settlement of their grievances. The Commission itself may, in time, have to play some such role. Already it has initiated seminars and a study of minority cultures[19] and education in bilingual regions.[20] These constructive contributions to rational discussion of a pan-European issue might usefully be augmented by a series of empirical studies of such subjects as mass media provision for minority language communities and an examination of the economies which support such cultures.

There are other forums and institutions through which linguistic minorities can seek to advance their interests. The

Helsinki agreement contains references[21] to 'cultural rights', the rights of 'national minorities' and pledges of support for 'less widely spoken languages' and 'national minorities or regional cultures' in various cultural endeavours. It is not yet possible to discover if any of these clauses have been availed of at Belgrade by linguistic minorities seeking redress.

In October 1977 the Parliamentary Assembly of the Council of Europe adopted a recommendation on modern languages in Europe.[22] The debate took place on the basis of the Picket Report which stated:

> Although we need to develop the knowledge of foreign languages, and in particular those which are widely used, we must also respect and protect the languages and dialects of small communities for, as I have already said, it is in Europe's cultural diversity that its richness lies. The great number of ways in which, at regional and local levels, efforts have been made to defend and protect threatened cultures is quite striking. In our own member states we have cultural associations set up to keep alive and develop such minority languages as Sardinian, Basque, Breton, Alsatian, Frisian and Welsh. An overall European policy would mean that we could bring order to a sector where lack of concerted policies could well produce dangerous explosions of regionalism or nationalism. We can therefore consider ourselves fortunate that on 8 July 1977 the Standing Committee, acting on behalf of the Assembly, adopted Order No. 364 which asked the Committee on Culture and Education to produce a specific study of minority languages and dialects. This investigation is to take into account the position adopted by the governments which signed the Final Act of Helsinki, which recognised the contribution which national minorities and regional cultures can make to co-operation. Similar concern was also expressed in the Galway Declaration of 1975.[23]

The recommendation adopted had the following two references supportive of minority interests:

> 2. Being of the opinion that cultural diversity is an irreplaceable asset, and that this justifies the active maintenance of language minorities in Europe;

and

9. Recommends that the Committee of Ministers:

   a) Call on the governments of the member states of the Council of Europe to develop the teaching of modern languages, taking account of: . . .

   (iii) the cultural advantages of maintaining language minorities in Europe.

The debate afforded a rare opportunity to an organised lobby to have specific grievances of particular minority groups identified and the failure of national governments to accommodate them placed on the official record. It was an opportunity missed. Only one speaker, quoted below, was critical of the lack of general action on the ground and identified a specific case.

> The report refers constantly to 'the rich pattern of language throughout Europe', but it concentrates too much on the majority languages, even though it makes reference to opposing any hierarchy of European languages. We have been faced in recent years with obligatory references on the subject from the Council of Ministers, the Helsinki Final Act, the Galway meeting and in the subsequent Galway Declaration, on the need to encourage the linguistic minorities, but the words have not always been matched by subsequent action at ministerial level . . .
>
> My own party, and similar parties throughout Europe, would certainly wish to see much more emphasis put on the retention of such languages to ensure, as my party wants in Scotland, that the indigenous *An Comunn Gaidlealach* is given official status, and that all speakers of Gaelic, whether native or acquired, are free to use their own language in all aspects of social, political and religious life . . .[24]

CONCLUSIONS

The peoples of Europe are beginning to be persuaded of the merits of supporting minority languages but more concerted and vigorous action is required by the minorities themselves to promote a common policy that will be applied. A determined regional policy is unlikely in the near future.

Economic intervention to halt decline in the peripheral areas may have a perverse effect on a minority language depending upon the way in which such a policy is implemented.

Job creation in local economies or the introduction of the vernacular or bilingualism into the educational system tends to have an impact on the wider minority community over the medium-term.

Expansion and improvement in vernacular mass media provision can have a widely dispersed impact in the short run.

NOTES

1. John Montague, 'A Severed Head' from: *The Rough Field* (Dublin: Dolman Press, 1974).
2. George Steiner, 'The Tongues of Men', *The Listener*, 28 April 1977.
3. Faroe Isles population: 38,731 (1972); Iceland: 218,000 (1974).
4. Steiner, *op. cit.*
5. Peripheral linguistic minorities in the EEC: the Celtic minorities of the British Isles and France, *viz.* the Gaels of Ireland and Scotland, the Welsh, and the Bretons; the Basque and Catalan minorities of France; the Eskimos of Greenland; the Frisians of the Netherlands and the Federal German Republic; the speakers of Corsican and Sard on their respective islands and the Ladins and Friulans of Italy.
6. See R. Petrella, 'Economic Development and Cultural "Minorisation"', *International Developments, Regional Policies and Territorial Identities in Western Europe*, an International study initiated by Professor Stein Rokkan, University of Bergen.
7. A. E. Alcock, *Protection of Minorities* (Northern Ireland Constitutional Convention, Belfast, 1975), p. 51.
8. Galway (Ireland) 1975, the regions represented were: Apulia, Aquitaine, Basilicata, Bavaria, *Land* Berlin, Brittany, Corsica, Cyprus, Emilia-Romagna, England, Friuli-Venezia Giulia, Greece, *Land* Hamburg, Iceland, Languedoc-Roussillon, Marche, Midi-Pyrénées, Lower Normandy, North Jutland, Norway, Pays de la Loire, Poitou-Charentes, Sardinia, *Land* Lower Saxony, *Land* Schleswig-Holstein, Scotland, Sicily, Veneto, Wales. *Bulletin of the Council of Europe* 3/75.
9. J. I. Prattis, *Economic Structures in the Highlands of Scotland* (Glasgow: Frazer of Allander Institute, 1977).
10. Meic Stephens, *Linguistic Minorities in Western Europe* (Llandysul, Gomer Press, 1976).
11. *Comharchumann Chois Fharraige*, Connemara, Irish Republic.
12. Professor Kenneth Alexander, Chairman of the Highlands and Islands Board, Press Release (9 November, 1977).
13. A. Campbell and B. Foster, 'The Mondragon Movement, Industrial Common Ownership Movement', Pamphlet no. 5 (London, 1974), p. 12.

14. Meic Stephens, *op. cit.*, pp. 543–52.
15. A. E. Alcock, *The History of the South Tyrol Question* (London: Michael Joseph, 1970), p. 238.
16. A. E. Alcock, *Protection of Minorities, op. cit.*
17. The address is: The Secretary, 13 Rue Hobbema, 1040, Brussels.
18. The Secretary of the League is: Alan Heusaff, 9 Bothar Cnoc Sion, Baile Atha Cliath 9, Ireland.
19. R. Petrella, *The Regions of Europe* (Document x/467/76F/ Brussels, July 1976).
20. Price, Hostert, Molitor-Funck. A comparative study on programmes, schedules and methods in use in bilingual regions and in schools offering bilingual education to foreign children. To be published by the EEC Directorate for Research, Science and Education.
21. *Conference on Security and Co-operation in Europe—Final Act* (Helsinki, 1975), pp. 80/vii, 108–9, 123, 126, 130, 131.
22. Council of Europe, *Recommendation 814* (1977) (1), Committee on Culture and Education.
23. F. Picket (rapporteur), *Report on Modern Languages in Europe* (Brussels, Council of Europe, 1977).
24. See the Council of Europe's official report; As(29)CR7 (October 1977). UK speaker, G. Reid.

6 The Development of Governmental Attitudes to Cultural Minorities in Western Industrial States

Antony E. Alcock

There are over twenty-five cultural minorities in the western industrial world today individually sufficiently numerous and having the will to ensure that their separate characteristics are maintained and developed.[1] In addition, four states acknowledge the multicultural principle as the basis for their existence.[2]

The former group can be divided into three categories: those that enjoy harmonious relations with the cultural majority of the state of which they are citizens, like the Aland Islanders; those that are achieving a satisfactory relationship with the majority only after many years of strife, such as the South Tyrolese; and those for whom harmonious relations with the majority are still a long way off, such as Bretons, Corsicans and Basques, who inhabit countries like France where the principles of cultural centralism are very strongly entrenched.

In 1950 Terence Harrington Bagley wrote that in states in which the government was a political and economic structure and not concerned with questions of nationality, such as France and Great Britain, there was no distinction made either in law or in fact between minorities and the rest of the population. The same rights applied to all and each cultural or ethnic group was free to continue its own traditions and customs within the political framework of the state. Such ethnic groups as existed—and Bagley named the Basques, Bretons, Alsatians and Scots—had no desire to be regarded as 'minorities' with special status and special aspirations. It was simply not in their interest to be so regarded. With the assurance of their rights, and the fulfilment of their cultural aspirations within the state, members of such groups tended to identify themselves first with the state and only secondarily with the more restricted community of ethnic or linguistic or religious unity of which they were members.[3]

Much has happened since these words were written, and the views held have been largely, although not entirely, contradicted by events. A review of the situation of cultural minorities in the western industrial world today shows that strife between cultural majorities and minorities has become just as fierce in those cases where minorities enjoy equality of rights with the majorities and there is no distinction made between them in law or fact and where minorities have almost complete control of their cultural destiny, as in cases where special measures of protection, whether at the national or international level, could be held to weaken the union between minorities and the host state.

If this has been the fundamental development in majority-minority relations since the Second World War, why has it happened? Why is attention now being focused on Bretons, Basques, Scots, Welsh, Catalans and French Canadians? What lessons are to be learned from the histories of the Aland Islands, South Tyrol and Cyprus that can shed light on this change?

The answers are to be found in the changes that have taken place in regard to the quality, nature and locus of minority protection, changes which themselves arise out of general economic, political and social development of western society itself, and in particular the relationship between government and the citizen.

Regarding the quality of protection, international instruments dealing with minority protection before the First World War were concerned to see that there should be no civil or political discrimination against citizens who belong to religious minorities.[4] Then between the wars certain minorities were granted so-called 'negative' and 'positive' rights. The former were rights similar to those enjoyed by all citizens, such as the right for the minority to use its language in private commerce, press, meeting and religion, and to establish private schools, while the latter referred to special rights granted to the individual members of the minority with the object of helping them maintain and develop their special characteristics. These included the right to use their language on certain public, as opposed to private occasions, such as in the courts; the right to receive instruction in their own language in state primary schools in those towns and districts where members of the minority formed a considerable proportion of the population, as well as the right to an equitable share in public funds for education, religious or charitable purposes.[5]

However, as a result of the widely held feeling that the granting of special 'positive' rights to German cultural minorities had prevented the latter's integration into their various host states and that an important cause of the Second World War had been Nazi exploitation of this failure to integrate, there was a general reluctance after 1945 to continue providing minorities with special 'positive' rights, and instead it was considered that all countries should maintain a universal standard of human rights which would provide individual members of a minority with protection against discrimination on ethnic, religious, linguistic or racial grounds and that it should be up to the state concerned to decide whether or not to grant its minorities any special 'positive' rights.[6] This reversion to the concept of 'negative' rights as the best for protecting minorities was reinforced by the view that in any case a government which violated the basic human rights of its ordinary citizens would be unlikely to respect special rights for its minorities.[7] And indeed on only four subsequent occasions did the great powers intervene to see that states provided special rights for minorities.[8]

Regarding the nature of protection, there has been an expansion in the fields in which minorities are seeking protection. From the prohibition of discrimination on religious grounds up to the outbreak of the First World War, to the granting of 'negative' and 'positive' rights in the cultural field between the wars, cultural protection has now come to be accepted, by and large, by host states in the western world.

This is certainly the case where minorities have kin-states, and can be attributed directly to the decline of the nation-state and the rise of national interdependence, in the west. The close relations between the member states of western Europe, for example, has led to the mutual acceptance of high cultural values and high standards of human rights through adherence to the instruments of the Council of Europe and in particular, the European Convention on Human Rights and Fundamental Freedoms, 1950. This has greatly diminished the possibilities for minorities successfully to cause political trouble between states on grounds of direct cultural discrimination by the host state. The problem today, therefore, is not that minorities seek protection for their cultural values against deliberately hostile actions by the majority in the field of schools and language, so much as the desire for protection against the effects on their culture of natural economic and social developments.

Likewise, even where cultural minorities have no kin-state, as is the case with minorities in France, Spain and Britain, and where the struggle is concentrated on the attempt to gain the same high degree of cultural freedom as has been achieved elsewhere in Europe by national minorities the same concern with the effect of natural economic and social development is to be noted.

Regarding the locus of protection, originally it had been the desire of the international community, as expressed by the great powers, to prevent international complications arising out of the transfer of groups of people from the authority of one state to that of another against their will that had sparked the idea of protection of minorities. Before the First World War it was the great powers that had required that certain host states should not discriminate against religious minorities as a condition either of their recognition or acceptance of an increase in their territory. And the opportunity was provided for individual great power intervention in case of a breach of obligations by the host state. Between the Wars it was the great powers again that required certain host states to provide their minorities with 'positive' and 'negative' cultural rights either as a condition of their entry into the League of Nations, or (as Clemenceau stated in his famous letter to Paderewski answering the complaint that the imposition of the Minorities Treaties was a breach of state sovereignty and equality for the states concerned) because it was due to the efforts of the great powers on the Allied side that these states owed their existence or increased their territory, and the great powers felt that the chief burden for the maintenance of peace lay with them. It was therefore not unreasonable for them to see that possible reasons for disturbances of world peace should be removed.[9] And the great powers accordingly set up machinery under the League of Nations both to deal with petitions from minorities regarding their treatment, and to settle disputes between the host and kin-states arising out of that treatment.

However, after the Second World War, because of the widespread feeling that minorities should not receive any special rights, that all countries should maintain a universal standard of human rights, and that it should be up to the state concerned to grant its minorities any special rights, as well as the return to the principles of state equality and sovereignty, as expressed by Article 2, paragraph 7, of the United Nations Charter, the great powers neither continued the League of Nation's machinery to supervise protection of minorities, nor revised it. Instead, they sought to have the international machinery of the United Nations used to see that individual members of a minority were not subject to discrimination, even though the extent of that organisation's capacity to intervene in cases of discrimination by a host state clearly rested with that state itself.[10]

The picture that then emerges is that it is upon the state that the onus for deciding on the quality and nature of minority protection has come overwhelmingly to lie.

These events occurred at a time when western society was increasing in numbers and becoming ever more dependent on industrial technological development. If the rate of population increase in the west was still much lower than elsewhere, nevertheless housing and jobs, in other words, living and working space, has had to be found for the newcomers. The result has been the development of a society overwhelmingly urbanised, technologically oriented and requiring a high degree of skills, with its members having to become increasingly mobile, both occupationally and residentially, in order to take advantage of what it has to offer. For the individual, however, this has been a mixed blessing. If living standards have risen, education has become more widely available, career possibilities have increased in scope, quantity and quality, and the time for leisure increased, the other side of the coin is the danger of losing social roots, weakening family ties, and alienation of one's origins.

For governments in the west these developments have created serious problems of co-ordination and control. Inevitably, they see themselves as arbiters of the rate and direction of change in their national societies. But the complex international interdependence of economic and social factors has weakened their ability to get to grips at the national level with the varied crises that have been occurring with such frequency and whose effects have been so long-lasting and pervasive, such as overpopulation, underemployment, inflation and shortages in raw materials. On the other hand, their very questionable belief that they know all the answers and therefore have a right to act as social engineers, has led them, despite their record, and despite their decline in capability and authority, to acquire even more responsibilities and powers, thus inevitably increasing their intervention, not only in the number of economic and social activities, but also in the daily lives of their citizens. This has been achieved through a massive increase in the output of legislation and an appropriate increase in the number of civil servants to administer it. Paradoxically, however, the more governments have intervened in the lives of their citizens the more distant from them they have become, since the less has been their need to heed. The bureaucratic apparatus of the state stands between the individual citizen and the makers of the decisions that govern his life. His ability to influence those decisions has declined as swiftly as the capability and authority of the government at whose knee he presses his suit. It should not be surprising that so many have begun to switch their loyalty from seemingly unresponsive national government to institutions more accessible or effective, if these exist, or to call for them if they do not. On the other hand, faced with the complexity of daily life, and aware of the growing disenchantment with their performance, national governments have sought the answers in simplification and uniformity. Thus the nation's citizens are considered as having the same social and economic aspirations and are treated on a basis of equality: equality before the law and equality before the administration. Furthermore, equality in the application of economic and social policies governs the government's approach. The general interest tends to be considered in terms of numbers in deciding political, economic and social priorities, and the whole of the national territory is considered to be available for the application of policies in these fields.

What is causing the crisis in majority–minority relations today is that minorities are questioning all these criteria for state behaviour. They are denying that a point of departure based on equality for all is the appropriate way of treating their own special problems, and they are challenging the assumption that the state's overall, centralist and equalitarian approach to economic and social problems is relevant to their aspirations.

Before considering these aspirations and how they are being imperilled, two points need to be made. First of all, many governments and indeed most people, are inclined to see the existence of different cultures within a nation and the existence of systems which seem to separate these different cultures as divisions which in themselves are a source of conflict. Equally, they tend to think of cultural assimilation as a process that is either generally desirable or in any case inevitable, and certainly one that should not be interfered with. But the fact of the matter is that *it is the exact opposite which is true.* The point about culturally divided societies—in South Tyrol, Cyprus, Canada, Belgium, Lebanon, *is that they wish to remain divided.* Each group draws the essence of its being, its group consciousness, from the fact that it *is* different and that it *wishes to remain different.* Those who see division as a source of conflict overlook that conflict arises because of threats to the factors which make for that division—threats to the separate identity, characteristics or even existence of the group, whether these threats be active (such as physical or cultural genocide or discriminatory legislation) or passive (such as non-recognition of the group or benign neglect by the majority of the effects on the minority of economic, social or technological change or pressure.

Second, it is of course, upon a minority's cultural power that its ability to express and maintain an identity distinct from that of the majority depends. But what is the source of cultural power? And is it right to talk in terms of 'power' at all?

There are many—particularly from the cultural majority—who will argue that it is quite wrong to talk of 'power' when referring to the culture of minorities and that separate cultural identity can be quite adequately assured by setting up the appropriate programmes to foster cultural differences, with teaching in the mother tongue, publication of newspapers, books and journals, as well as broadcasting and television in the language of the minority, the restoration and maintenance of objects of historical and archival interest, and the promotion of folklore-type activities (usually for the benefit of tourists). The corollary is that it is immaterial whether these facilities are controlled by the majority or the minority.

This is to take the view that all that is needed is for the minority culture to be tolerated and for the institution of the appropriate cultural instruments to do the rest.

Only a little thought is needed to realise that this by itself cannot be sufficient. If it is true that the culture of a minority is the outward expression of a community group of individuals which is conscious of having an identity different from that of the majority group in the state, it is equally true that the will to retain such a separate identity—the fount from which all minority protection flows—implies that the aspirations of the two—majority and minority—will also be different. They may share—or have been forced to share—the same political framework; but this does not mean that they share a common destiny—an assumption all too blithely accepted by the majority. On the contrary, it is precisely the feeling of members of the minority that they have a different destiny that is the mainspring of the will to retain their separate identity. Thus the destiny of a minority is not linked solely to its ability to maintain its separate cultural characteristics but also to its ability to maintain itself as a group—and that means politically, economically and socially *vis-à-vis* the rest of the world in general, but more particularly, *vis-à-vis* the host state.

The two factors are complementary, and cultural minorities are only too aware that failure to maintain themselves politically, economically and socially leads to erosion of cultural identity. This is one of the main lessons of the crisis in Quebec where, although the province is autonomous in cultural matters, failure to develop and keep pace economically and socially with anglophone North American dynamism, as expressed through natural economic development, endangered French culture.[11]

Cultural power may therefore be expressed as the ability of a culture to maintain itself in a world of rapid social and technological change. This means that a cultural minority must be able to develop itself at least so as to keep pace and compete with the host state majority at the economic and social level, and this in turn means that when one talks of 'protection' of minorities it is not merely a question of introducing measures that would preserve minorities, like flies, in amber, but that their ability to develop themselves will be an inherent part of the process of protection.

But upon what does the ability to do this—the source of cultural power—depend? The short answer is that cultural power depends on economic power, but economic power is itself composed of two elements.

The first of these is a factor which has tended to be overlooked in consideration of minority problems, namely, the land itself upon which a minority dwells.

In the western world, most cultural minorities have a homeland. They may be a majority in that homeland or even a minority there, but in either case that area is the land upon which they live and their ancestors have lived for centuries. That land and the natural resources contained therein is their economic heritage. Agricultural, industrial or touristic, or a combination of these, it is, for better or worse, for richer or poorer, the motor for their cultural power and the motor upon which will depend their ability to keep pace with the majority, resist the latter's economic and social pressures and survive the challenges of natural economic and social development. But if power is expressed by the combination and mobilisation of resources to control others, and it is the cultural majority that controls resources then it also controls the life chances of the minority, especially the terms on which the minority have access to resources, jobs, education, and wealth. In that the minority will thus be dependent on the majority for the rate at which it develops and the level of development which it attains, the relationship between majority and minority will be like a colonial one.[12]

If the natural resources contained in the land upon which the minority dwells is the basis for their economic power, then the likelihood is that there will be competition between the majority, representing the state and the national interest as a whole, and the minority, for those resources. This in turn, raises the question of the ability of the minority to defend its land in that competition, and introduces the second element of economic power, namely, the social composition of the minority.

In order both to exploit the resources of its homeland and to keep pace and compete with the majority, the minority must be sufficiently flexible in its social composition. That is to say, it must be balanced in order to meet the demands of local economy. All too often minorities are over-represented in one sector, usually agriculture, and under-represented in others. This causes two further problems: if the sector is declining, how to absorb those leaving the sector into other sectors; and how to avoid having members of the majority come to take employment in sectors where the minority is under-represented.

Since one of the pillars of minority protection is that the minority in question must have the will to preserve in order to benefit from protection, it is not surprising that this will is expressed by a determination not to be involved in a colonial situation and not to rely on the majority for the rate and level of its development but rather to control its destiny by being in charge of these factors itself. Consequently if the sources of a minority's cultural and economic power, namely, its homeland and social composition, begin to be eroded then the relations between the minority and the host state will become acute.

But what has so far been underestimated is the degree to which the principle of equality of human rights and non-discrimination, particularly in the economic field, can contribute to the erosion process.

Two examples, both in the field of employment, spring to mind. The first of these is liberty of movement and freedom to choose one's place of residence. Not only is this right enshrined in most national constitutions, but it is also contained in Article 13 of the (non-binding) Universal Declaration of Human Rights; Article 12 of the United Nations Covenant on Civil and Political Rights; and Protocol 4 of the European Convention on Human Rights; while liberty of movement and residence in order to take up work anywhere in the Common Market is laid down in Article 48 of the Treaty of Rome.

This means that in most states, and in any country ratifying the above-mentioned binding instruments, members of the cultural majority will have the right to go and live and seek work in the homeland of a cultural minority.

The reason for such immigration may be entirely honourable: to participate in the expansion of a sector of the economy in the area, or to participate in the development of an entirely new sector, such as the exploitation of newly-discovered raw materials. But as previously mentioned, if the minority does not have the manpower, skilled or otherwise, or the finance, to participate in that development, then the vacuum will be filled by members of the majority. This highlights the importance of vocational education and technical skill, and the need for social flexibility since the danger that members of the majority will come swarming into the minority's homeland and upset its ethnic and cultural nature is very real and has ample precedents.[13] However, there are other aspects of the immigration factor that need to be considered.

One of these is that the arrival in the minority's homeland of large numbers of another cultural group may cause social conflict because of the possibility of mixed marriages. The minority will see this as something to weaken the cultural cohesion of the group; on the other hand, any active opposition to mixed marriages by the minority will lay it open to charges by the majority of discrimination and hostility to human rights that will only exacerbate existing majority-minority animosity.

The other side of the coin is that a minority which has no control over the economic forces in its land nor has the social ability to compete with the majority may see itself weakened by emigration. This may well happen if facilities are not adequate to retrain members of the minority leaving a declining sector, such as agriculture, so that they can be absorbed by other sectors.

Whether through immigration of members of the majority or emigration of members of the minority, it will be increasingly difficult to defend the homeland and the danger—particularly in areas of mixed population—is that the numbers of the minority will decline to such an extent that its position in terms of local politics and government will be adversely affected. Indeed, little does a minority view with greater concern than being turned into a minority also in its own homeland.

In this regard even in those regions where the decline in the agricultural sector has been offset by another post-second-war trend, namely, the development of tourism, this has been something of a mixed blessing. If it provides a source of income, then it is likely to do so only seasonally. There are few regions as fortunate as South Tyrol with facilities for tourism all the year around. Moreover, tourism has also been considered dangerous in that it introduces an alien element into communities struggling to keep their own identity. A particular concern has been the phenomenon of second, or holiday homes owned by members of the host majority. They are a source of resentment on two counts—as intruders, first, and then as users of resources for the building of their homes when these resources might be better used to build new, or improve, homes for the minority.[14]

The second example of equality of human rights eroding the minority culture in the homeland occurs in the public administration. In almost all national constitutions, in the Universal Declaration of Human Rights, and in the United Nations Covenant on Civil and Political Rights the principle is established of equality in access to employment in the public administration. Interestingly, this principle is not mentioned in the European Convention on Human Rights.

It should be obvious that the public administration in a minority's homeland must be more than a question of mere administration. It also has cultural, economic and social significance.

Culturally, members of the minority wish to see their own kind administering their land. They wish to be able to use their own language in speech and in writing when communicating with the public authorities and receiving replies. Economically, employment in the public service is important since it provides jobs—relatively well-paid, secure and pensionable jobs. This is crucial if the minority as a whole is economically worse off than the majority. Socially, in that the public service provides jobs, it is an important element in providing the employment balance the minority needs in order to obtain the flexibility referred to earlier.

For all these reasons minorities prefer to see the principle of proportional representation used in the public service, and that it will apply not only to the local government of the homeland but also to jobs in those branches of the central or federal government that have their offices in the homeland.

The problem is that the principle of proportional representation is difficult to equate with that of equality of rights. It offends against the merit principle, and has been a source of grievance.[15] On the other hand, it will be difficult for cultural minorities to have members of their group get jobs at all, particularly at higher career levels, if, with their often very small percentage of the total national population, their candidates have to compete on terms of equality, against candidates from the whole country. They argue, therefore, that the only way to ensure that their candidates obtain places would be to reserve a certain percentage for them.

Another aspect of this problem is that civil servants are often transferred during the course of their career to other parts of the country, especially the national capital. Minorities are therefore keen to see that members of their group employed in the civil service, with the obvious exceptions of the Foreign Service and Ministry of Defence, are kept *en poste* in the homeland. This particularly applies to the police.[16]

If the application of the principle of equality of human rights can—and has—led to the erosion of the homelands of cultural minorities, then hopes of having the host state governments devolve economic and social power to minorities to the degree necessary to protect their homeland and attain social flexibility have tended to founder on what Patricia Mayo has condemned as the quality of much of contemporary government and the philosophy on which it is based, namely, dogmatic centralism and the 'passion' for social uniformity shared by the bureaucrat and the orthodox European left. To the bureaucrat a uniform society simplified administration while to the socialist it was synonymous with social justice.[17]

One feature that cultural minorities share to a surprisingly large degree is that their homelands are to be found among the poorer regions of host states, particularly rural regions. In these cases, therefore, the two causes, economic and social protection of minorities to strengthen their cultural characteristics, and economic and social development of backward regions, come to be linked.

However, all too rarely does the government's approach take into account the danger of the latter to the former and seek to reconcile the two causes. All too often it is the latter cause which gets priority, and all too often the government's approach to regional development is based on equalitarianism and uniformism in the interest of equality of standards. This 'makes it difficult for the central government to permit autonomy at regional levels where this threatens to create a geographic variation of public services'.[18]

For example, when nationalist parties in Scotland and Wales complained of Westminster's uniform management of the economy, they pointed out that when the south-east of the United Kingdom was fully employed economic expansion had to stop in homelands. They called for revenue raising and expenditure powers to stimulate the economy at the regional level and thus help iron out regional disparities, but it was argued that although this idea was attractive to many economists, 'there are thought to be political difficulties in increasing further disparities in public expenditure *per capita*, and it is also thought that it would be unacceptable to the majority of people if taxes are to be charged at different rates in different parts of the United Kingdom.[19]

Other common complaints by minorities are, first, that where the regional homeland of the minority possesses natural resources, if these are understandably exploited by the central government in the interests of the nation as a whole, nevertheless the revenues from these resources are inadequately ploughed back into the area for the benefits of the inhabitants, and that the resources themselves are often not made widely and cheaply available to the local population.[20] Second, that individual and corporate taxation systems are such that despite the relative poverty of these regions, national governments get more out of them financially than they put in in the form of tax incentives to firms and infrastructure development spending.[21] Third, even if these regions have developed legislative powers and financial resources of their own, these are usually inadequate to deal with the problems involved, and the regional authority then has to rely on funds from the central government which provides opportunities for the latter to carry out plans despite—or even contrary—to the wishes of the regional authority.[22]

Much of the foregoing has been devoted to the theme of equality and its effects on the desire of cultural minorities to control their own destinies. But to what extent is the basis of the arguments for equality valid?

Here a distinction must be made between equality in law and equality in fact. As the Permanent Court of International Justice stated in its Advisory Opinion regarding Minority Schools in Albania:

> For minorities to live on equal terms with the majority it would be necessary for them to have the juridical, social, economic and cultural institutions to allow them to cultivate and develop their own language and culture under the same conditions as the majority.
> Equality in *law* precludes discrimination of any kind, whereas equality in *fact* may involve the necessity of different treatment in order to attain a result which establishes an equilibrium between different situations.

In the case in question, the Albanian government had closed down all private schools in the country and argued that since this applied to the private schools of the Albanian majority and the Greek minority alike, no discrimination was involved. In its Opinion, which was adopted by 8 votes to 3, the Court held that the Albanian government's action was incompatible with Article 5 of the Declaration of the Albanian government to the League of Nations that nationals belonging to racial, religious, or linguistic minorities should 'enjoy the same treatment and security in law and in fact as other Albanian nationals'.

The three dissenting judges argued that were the Greek minority to have a right (i.e. to keep their private schools open) which was unconditional and independent of that enjoyed by others, it could not be described as equal. Was the intention of the Declaration therefore to grant to the minority an *unconditional* right to maintain and establish these schools? The Court, in its Opinion, answered this question in the affirmative.[23] The reason is easy to find. Whereas the Albanian government was quite free to decide on the measures necessary for the maintenance of the majority culture, the Greek minority did not have that same freedom. Therefore, the cultivation and development of their language and culture could not 'take place under the same conditions as the majority', and different treatment would be needed to bring those same conditions about.

The same problem of the meaning of *de facto* equality arose in South Tyrol after the Second World War. In their Memorandum to the Italian government in April 1954, the leaders of the South Tyrolese stated that for the protection of minorities one needed equality, but this equality must be more than formal. It must also be effective, and this meant that the minority should have the faculty and possibility of satisfying its own interests, and spiritual, cultural, economic, administrative and political needs with means as effective as those used by the majority.

The Memorandum continued with these immortal words: 'There is no greater inequality than to treat equally unequal things. Therefore special laws to protect a minority are not privileges but measures to create this material equality between majority and minority.'

And the South Tyrolese pointed out not only that the Italian Constitution provided in Article 6 for the protection of minorities through special measures, but also that certain general constitutional rights, including the movement of the citizen in the territory of the Republic, could be limited when higher interest demanded it.[24]

In conclusion, there are signs that governmental attitudes to cultural minorities in western industrial states have slowly begun to shift. There has been a growing awareness of the difficulties cultural minorities face in the vortex of industrial society, although this has not led anywhere to the appropriate action being taken.

On the one hand, satisfaction has not been obtained for those who see salvation in formal recognition of the right to their homeland and the right to have its ethnic character maintained, and, on the basis of this and recognition of the link binding them to past and future generations, having protection of the individual member of the group extended to the group as a whole.

On the other hand, pressure to bring about that degree of devolved government to ensure better cultural protection seems to have succeeded, as in South Tyrol and the *Jura bernois*, or seems to be about to succeed, as in Catalonia and Wales. At the same time, some countries, like Italy and Spain, have begun to decentralise, and even in those like France that have not decentralised, there are now wider opportunities for studying minority cultures in the education system and wider access to the media, although in these fields there is obviously still a very long way to go.

The day when cultural minorities will be satisfied with their position in the nation state will come nearer when governments perceive them not merely as citizens but also as co-founders of the nation in which they dwell, so that charge of the future of the nation becomes a multicultural endeavour.

NOTES

1. 38,000 Rhaetians (Ladins) in Switzerland.
   50,000 Lapps in Norway, Sweden and Finland.
   310,000 Frisians in the Netherlands, West Germany and Denmark.
   350,000 Swedes in Finland (including the Aland islanders).
   110,000 Germans in Belgium.
   23,000 Germans and 37,000 Faroe islanders in Denmark.
   50,000 Danes in West Germany.
   90,000 Basques, 3,200,000 Bretons, 1,200,000 Alsatians, 1,150,000 Occitans, 190,000 Corsicans and 200,000 Flemings in France.
   2,600,000 Welsh and 5,000,000 Scots in Great Britain and 500,000 Catholics in Northern Ireland.
   250,000 South Tyrolese, 60,000 Val d'Aostans, 25,000 Ladins, 800,000 Friulans, 1,200,000 Sardinians in Italy.
   25,000 Slovenes in Austria.
   40,000 Finns in Sweden.
   525,000 Basques, 2,619,000 Galicians and 8,500,000 Catalonians in Spain.
   1,500,000 Indians in the United States, and Canada.
   M. Straka, *Handbuch der Europäischen Volksgruppen* (Vienna, 1970), pp. 54–9; R. Petrella, *Les Régions et l'Europe* (Brussels, Commission of the European Communities, Doc. X/467/1/76 of September 1976), pp. 100 ff; Minority Rights Group, *Series of Reports* (London, 1971–7).
2. Belgium, Canada, Cyprus and Switzerland.
3. T. H. Bagley, *General Principles and Problems in the International Protection of Minorities* (Geneva, 1950), pp. 16–17.
4. For example, the Protocol to the Treaty of Paris (1856) regarding Moldavia and Wallachia; the Treaty of Berlin (1878) regarding the independence of Rumania, Serbia, Montenegro and the autonomy of Bulgaria; the Greco-Turkish Treaty of Constantinople (1881).
5. For example, the so-called Minorities Treaties between the Principal Allied and Associated Powers and Poland (28 June 1919), Czechoslovakia and Yugoslavia (10 September 1919), Rumania (9 December 1919) and Greece

(10 August 1920); the final peace with Turkey, signed at Lausanne (24 July 1923), and Declarations made by Finland (27 June 1921), Albania (2 October 1921), Lithuania (12 May 1922), Latvia (7 July 1923), Estonia (17 September 1923) and Iraq (30 May 1923) on becoming members of the League of Nations.

6. Undoubtedly this attitude was helped by the fact that with the decision at Potsdam (August 1945) to expel the German minorities in Poland and Czechoslovakia, and the displacement of frontiers, there were fewer minorities to protect. In any case the Peace Treaties with the Axis powers included a general article providing that the country concerned would take all necessary measures to ensure that everyone within its jurisdiction, without distinction as to race, sex, language or religion, enjoyed fundamental human rights and fundamental freedoms, including freedom of thought, press publication, culture, opinion and meeting.
   The best known examples of states granting special rights to minorities through national constitutions are the cases of Italy (with respect to the French-speaking population of Val d'Aosta) and Lebanon.
   States have also voluntarily concluded bilateral arrangements. The 1921 agreement between Sweden and Finland regarding the Aland islands, signed at the same time as the Finnish Declaration to the League of Nations, is still in force. More recently the status of Danish-speaking German citizens in *Land* Schleswig-Holstein, and German-speaking Danish citizens in the Province of North Schleswig has been regulated by the Bonn Declaration of 29 March 1955.
7. I. L. Claude, *National Minorities* (New York, 1955), pp. 56 ff.
8. These four relate to the Austro-Italian agreement of 5 September 1946 on South Tyrol, annexed to the Peace Treaty with Italy, 10 February 1947; the London agreement of 5 October 1954 on the Free Territory of Trieste, governing the status of Italians in the Yugoslav Zone and Yugoslavs in the Italian Zone; the Austrian State Treaty of 15 May 1955, and in particular Article 7 on the Slovene and Croat minorities; and the London and Zurich agreements of 1959 on the constitution of the Republic of Cyprus.
9. Partial text of the letter in P. de Azcaraté, *League of Nations and National Minorities* (New York: Kraus Reprint, 1972), pp. 166–7.
10. cf. Texts of the UN Convention on Civil and Political Rights and the Optional Protocol to the Convention (December 1966).
11. cf. *Report of the Royal Commission on Bi-lingualism and Bi-culturalism*, vol. 1, especially para 49 p. xxv (Ottawa, 1967).
12. cf. A. G. Dworkin and R. J. Dworkin, *The Minority Report* (New York, 1976), p. 20.
13. For example, German migration into former Danish Schleswig-Holstein and the mainly Polish Duchy of Posen in the 1860s; Italian migration into the Istrian peninsula, South Tyrol and Val d'Aosta between the wars encouraged by the Fascists; and migration from all parts of Spain into Catalonia encouraged by the regime of General Franco.
14. P. Mayo, *The Roots of Identity* (London, 1974), p. 91. Notable areas where second homes are a problem: Cornwall, Wales, Brittany, Val d'Aosta. In South Tyrol the Provincial government has made it very difficult for non-local inhabitants to acquire such property.

15. For example, Greek Cypriots complained bitterly that members of their community were being held back from jobs for which they were qualified in order that Turkish Cypriots, who, they claimed, were unqualified, could fill jobs in the basis of the proportional representation. An added source of grievance was that even proportional representation was not being observed in that under the Constitution of Cyprus, Turkish Cypriots, although only 18 per cent of the population, were being given 30 per cent of the posts.
A. E. Alcock, *Protection of Minorities—3 Case Studies: South Tyrol, Cyprus, Quebec* (Belfast: Northern Ireland Constitutional Convention, 1975).
16. The principle of proportional representation in the public administration is hardly accepted anywhere, although it is applied in some areas, notably in South Tyrol and Val d'Aosta, with respect to local government. In South Tyrol there is a struggle to get it accepted with .respect to national administrations with offices in the South Tyrolese homeland, the Province of Bolzano, such as the State Railways and the post and telegraph service. For the difficulties involved, see Alcock, *ibid.*, p. 14.
17. P. Mayo, *op. cit.*, pp. 1–2.
18. D. L. Coombes, 'Regionalism and Devolution in a European Perspective' in the Conference Papers, Rowntree Devolution Conference (Sunningdale, May 1976), p. 20.
19. C. Smallwood, 'Economic Aspects of Devolution' in Sunningdale Papers, *op. cit.*, p. 37.
20. For example, in South Tyrol and Brittany in regard to electricity developed from hydroelectric power.
21. See in this connection C. Morin, *Le Pouvoir Québecois en Négociation* (Quebec, 1972), in regard to Québec; D. Roy, *Les relations financières entre le Jura Sud et l'Etat de Berne* (La Neuveville, 1975), in regard to the problems of the *Jura bernois*; and P. Mayo, *op. cit.*, in regard to Wales.
22. As happened in regard to housing in South Tyrol. A. E. Alcock, *The History of the South Tyrol Question* (London, 1970), p. 315.
23. Advisory Opinion of 6 April 1935, PCIJ *Series A/B* no. 64.
24. A. E. Alcock, *op. cit.* (1970), pp. 238–9.

7 The Role of Law in Relation to Minority Groups*

Claire Palley

CONSTITUTIONAL DEVICES AND LEGAL ARRANGEMENTS

A convenient starting point for analysis of the effect of Law on minority groups is a catalogue of existing constitutional practices examined from the functional aspect, i.e. listed on the basis of who does what to whom.[1] Some passing reference is also made to the why, how, when and where of these practices. A functional catalogue of this sort takes as its point of departure the power groups controlling any state's machinery because power, combined with possible willingness to change state institutions or determination to maintain them, will be decisive for any outcome. Revolution apart, and bearing in mind the dominant groups' awareness of the inevitability of continuing relationships between themselves and other groups, it is the decisions of the current rulers (i.e. the elite of the dominant group) which will prevail. In the last resort they have 'the say' in deciding which policies shall be translated into law and legal institutions. In the context of a study of majority/minority group relations the functional aims will therefore be *integration* of the groups and individuals into the large society or *maintenance of differences* between groups and individuals in that society.

The techniques for furthering integration fall into two main categories: first, equality and non-discrimination techniques, usually labelled *assimilationist approaches*; and second *domination approaches*, where the integration is to be achieved by the imposition of the political, economic and cultural standards of the dominant group. In contrast, the *technique of pluralism* is usual where differences are sought to be maintained. Then groups will, in addition to their participation in some common and compulsory institutions, be permitted or accorded also 'alternative' or 'exclusive' institutions for particular purposes. If these arrangements are recognised by law there is formalised pluralism. If, in contrast, groups are not recognised *as such*, but institutional arrangements are made effectively to give a 'say' to the groups, without specifically designating them, then there is informal pluralism.[2] Seldom is one technique alone applied—the same elite may apply some assimilationist, some pluralist and some techniques of domination simultaneously.

ASSIMILATIONIST APPROACHES

The aim of such techniques is to eliminate differences of treatment between group and group, and individual and individual. Differences are not recognised by law—although there is usually an informal toleration of social groupings, and formal toleration to the extent that freedom of association is recognised by law. Assimilationist techniques create formal equality before the law, and, where group members have rights, it is in their individual capacities, and not as part of a majority or as part of a minority of the population. There are in fact two complementary principles involved in this approach: the first is the equality principle whereby all are to be treated equally; and the second is the non-discrimination principle, reinforcing the former by negative prohibitions on treating different persons in the same circumstances less favourably than other persons in those same circumstances are or would be treated.

An idea of the numerous techniques to secure equality and non-discrimination and ultimate assimilation can be obtained from the catalogue which follows:

1. *Bills of Rights*
   enumerating civil and political rights;
   conferring social, economic and cultural rights;
   protecting citizens only;
   protecting all persons within the jurisdiction;
   with or without judicial review to test constitutionality and for enforcement;
   with or without legal aid to assist aggrieved persons;
   with or without rigid procedures to stop easy amendment of the Bill;

an 'interpretation' Bill of Rights applying substantively so as to override earlier inconsistent legislation but as an Interpretation Act only in the case of future legislation in which event a later statute can expressly override the Bill of Rights (Canada).

2. *Non-justiciable Directive Principles of State Policy*
enunciation in the Constitution of general libertarian principles—serving as aids to interpretation—but not overriding earlier or later laws (Ireland, India and Pakistan).

3. *Special anti-discrimination constitutional provisions*
rendering laws and executive action contrary to them invalid (Government of Ireland Act 1920 sec. 5; Northern Ireland Constitution Act 1973).

4. *Anti-discrimination statutes*
with or without criminal sanctions;
with or without making 'incitement to discriminate' a criminal offence;
with or without civil actions in the ordinary courts for damages and injunctions to assist persons discriminated against;
with or without special tribunals to deal with employment grievances, e.g. discriminatory hiring, training, promotion, firing;
with administrative enforcement rather than direct enforcement by ordinary litigation in the Courts (e.g. consent of Attorney General a precondition to commencing enforcement action;
with conciliation machinery for parties to negotiate and settle their grievances;
with promotional machinery to promote good race relations in the community (e.g. Commission for Racial Equality UK);
with investigative machinery to investigate complaints of discrimination (e.g. Commission for Racial Equality UK);
with law reform machinery to make continuous surveys and to recommend changes to Parliament;
with power to deal with patterns of discrimination and to collect evidence;
with provision for modification or avoidance of discriminatory contractual terms.
(See generally Race Relations Act 1976 (UK); Race Rela-

tions Act 1971 (New Zealand); State Laws in many American States; Civil Rights Acts 1964 and 1968 (USA)).

5. *Franchise Laws*
   positive statements of voting rights;
   prohibitions on improper application of electoral laws e.g. by discrimination in voter registration procedures.
   (See generally Voting Rights Acts 1965, 1968 and 1970 (USA); Representation of the People Acts 1949 and 1969 (UK)).
6. *Constitutional protections for the enactment of certain laws (rigidity as opposed to flexibility)*
   special procedures specified in order to amend constitutional protections e.g. weighted majorities (say 2/3), or a referendum, and in federal states a requirement additionally of the assent of a majority of the regional units;
   specially entrenched provision requiring not merely the usual procedures for constitutional amendment but also additional safeguards (e.g. referendum with approval by a majority of each racial community voting separately as well as a specified majority in the legislature (Southern Rhodesia—here the safeguard is also pluralistic because it expressly recognises the groups));
   weighted majorities for ordinary legislation of specified character (Electoral Act in Southern Rhodesia);
   scrutiny of and reports on legislation by a specified body before final enactment and with a period of delay before legislation adversely reported on can be re-submitted to the legislature for enactment (Constitutional Council—Southern Rhodesia 1961–9);
   external controls such as enactment by an external body. (Certain constitutional amendment in Canada can be made only by the UK Parliament);
   external controls with Bills being reserved by a Governor and being submitted for Her Majesty's assent on United Kingdom Ministers' advice (Southern Rhodesia Constitution Order in Council 1961; all non-independent British Colonies).
7. *Special institutional arrangements to supervise the administration—thereby ensuring that governmental decisions are properly and fairly reached and are in accordance with principles of equality before the law and non-discrimination*

(a) 'Ombudsmen' responsible for investigating complaints about central government administration (Parliamentary Commissioner for Administration (UK); regional government administration (Parliamentary Commissioner for Administration (Northern Ireland); local government administration (Local Government Commissioners (England and Wales); Commissioner for Complaints (Northern Ireland); particular governmental functions (e.g. for health services in the UK)).

(b) Civil Service Commissions supervising the recruitment training, promotion and transfer of governmental employees 'independent' Commissions (many are in fact nominated, as in Zambia. Such Commissions are found in most former British possessions); regional Government Staff Commissions (Northern Ireland); Local Government Staff Commission (Northern Ireland).

8. *Special institutional arrangements in the private sphere to ensure that individuals are treated with equality and not discriminated against by other private individuals*

(a) Conciliation bodies whose main aim is to reconcile the parties and obtain undertakings that in future there will be no discriminatory conduct (Race Relations Board and local conciliation bodies under UK Race Relations Act 1968; anti-discrimination commissions as in various states of the USA);

(b) Promotional bodies who provide educational materials, do research, give advice/assistance to non-governmental organisations, report on desirable law reform and undertake investigations of alleged discrimination (Community Relations Commission under UK Race Relations Act 1968).

(c) Enforcement bodies

(Attorney-General under UK Race Relations Act 1965; Race Relations Board under UK Race Relations Act 1968; Commission for Racial Equality under UK Race Relations Act 1976 repealing earlier Acts; anti-discrimination commissions in various states of the USA).

(d) Specialised functional bodies concerned with private arrangements of major concern to society, e.g. fair employment bodies in the private sector to ensure fair and non discriminating employment practices (Fair Employment

Practices Commissions (states of USA); Fair Employment Commission (Northern Ireland 1976)).

9. *Judicial action i.e. enforcement machinery by litigation in the courts*
(a) constititional review (if provided in the constitution —India—or established by judicial rulings—USA);
(b) ordinary civil litigation and criminal proceedings in which the judges develop standards requiring non-discriminatory conduct;
(c) judicial review of administrative action when governmental decisions are challenged in the courts as being unlawful. Here judges have been inventive so as to require fair decision making by developing doctrines of public policy, presumptions of statutory interpretation including the rules of natural justice, and the doctrine of *ultra vires* so as to include discrimination. In the USA, with reliance on the constitution, the doctrine of judicial action as state action was invoked so as to refuse enforcement of discriminatory practices.

10. *Law enforcement machinery designed to secure equality and fairness under law*
(a) maintenance of a well trained police force with good disciplinary and grievance procedures;
(b) establishment of independent criminal prosecuting authorities who do not act at the behest of politicians;
(c) provision of safeguards for the accused in criminal procedures, both pre-trial and during the trial (evidentiary rules and procedural requirements).

11. *Executive action—to ensure fair decision making*
(a) imposition of high standards of training in administration;
(b) provision of appeal procedures in the administration (i) departmentally (ii) to an independent tribunal (iii) to an internal system of administrative courts;
(c) political and hierarchial supervision within the bureaucracy itself of bureaucratic conduct (whether at a central or a local government level).

12. *Parliamentary control—to ensure fairness, equality and non-discrimination, and justice*
various procedures including correspondence with ministers, questions, debates, select committee investigations involving problematic facts.

These techniques are designed to ensure good government in the sense of fairness, justice, equality and non-discrimination for all individuals and formally recognised group organisations (e.g. trade unions, clubs). They are certainly not designed to enhance or to reduce the relative power position of particular cultural groups. Nonetheless the cumulative effect of such measures is in the long run to integrate individuals and groups within the greater society, for individuals' group allegiance to fade, and for the relative influence of groups as a whole to be diminished. Competing claims for scarce resources then tend to be couched in individual, class, political, or economic terms rather than in the language of minority cultural group claims. Consequently, the minority cultural groups as such becomes less significant politically. Indeed, in an assimilationist society, the long run tendency is to political elimination of minority groups.

DOMINATION APPROACHES

Domination as a technique may be scaled along a range of attitudes from the most extreme position, where the majority group seeks absolute hegemony within the state, to situations where the elite of the dominant group is seeking to strengthen its own position relative to other groups by giving their own group members greater access to resources of political, economic and cultural power, or to situations where the aim is to maintain the *status quo* by supporting their own group's current power position.

There is little point in this chapter in dealing with states where the controlling elite have extreme domination or purification approaches. In such situations, if the power holders have sufficient force, they will exclude the minority groups by partition, or secession, or boundary redrawing, or by mass population expulsion whether directly imposed or indirectly ensured by the creation of intolerable living conditions for the minority. There may even be genocide. For the cultural minority within such a state there is no 'future'.

In the standard domination situation there are noticeable departures from the equality and non-discrimination principles. To the naive observer it is less obvious that when the *status quo* in a state is maintained there is equally domination in the form of an attempt to freeze existing power patterns. Failure by non-minority group members to perceive domination is even more frequent where existing state institutions do not formally recognise the cultural distinctiveness of minority communities. Such societies are often described as assimilationist. If the situation is analysed it is apparent that 'forced assimilation' is domination whether this is implemented by the provision only of majority-determined linguistic schooling or religious facilities, or by state preservation only of majority cultural symbols. It is domination in the sense of maintaining the current political, economic and cultural predominance of the majority group, and domination in that it denies alternatives to other groups whose members are subjected to enforced integration.

All departures from the equality and non-discrimination principles are not necessarily designed to confer economic and cultural benefits on the majority group and its members. Although this is the most frequent reason for departure from such principles, the dominant group's elite may instead adopt a strategy of destroying minority groups' motives for large scale political change by encouraging political stability through altering disadvantageous patterns of imbalance in the economic and cultural spheres as between different group members. (Many of the elite may have moral as opposed to merely Machiavellian motives.) In such an event legal arrangements will be used to improve the position of group members from the minority groups whose economic and social position has been selected for upgrading. Such a strategy to remedy imbalances resulting from preceding structural patterns in society is termed 'affirmative action'. This is discussed under the heading of domination, not merely because it is brought about by the same techniques used to further the interest of one group and its members as opposed to another, but because the following of such a policy is in essence coercive, being employed at the behest of the elite of the dominant group, which has decided to manipulate the positions of groups and individuals for whatever reason.

It is artificial to distinguish between institutional arrangements in the political, economic and cultural spheres, institutions being multi-faceted with impact in all spheres. It is equally artificial to distinguish institutional arrangements which shape ideology from those which are concerned with material force. Nonetheless for the purposes of exposition it is convenient to analyse domination techniques as being applied in four major spheres of the state action *viz.* the political, the economic, the cultural, and that of order backed by physical force. Within these spheres the legal techniques a dominating elite can select can be catalogued as set out below.

The political sphere The major technique employed to limit the political power of minority groups has been electoral manipulation. There are many variations. Potential voters may be disenfranchised by a combination of restrictive citizenship law and electoral law (Sri Lanka). A racial group may be disenfranchised by its removal from a common voters' roll combined with the provision of politically impotent new machinery (South Africa). There may be qualitative franchises, either with educational qualifications (southern states of the USA until the Voting Rights Act 1965) or income qualifications or a combination thereof (South Africa and Rhodesia) or property ownership or occupation (Northern Ireland local government franchise until 1969) or tax payment requirements (Rhodesia from 1969 to date). There may be voting registration procedures applied effectively against minority group members (USA until 1965 and Sri Lanka). There may be residential requirements to exclude potential supporters of the minority (Northern Ireland to preclude immigrants from the Irish Republic from voting in Northern Ireland elections for 7 years after arrival). There may be gerrymandering. There may be deliberate failure to redraw boundaries or to take account of demographic changes or to alter institutions when some provisions have disappeared, thereby frustrating the original purpose of the system (Northern Ireland local government elections until 1969—where the plural business vote favouring Protestants, multi-member constituencies designed for proportional representation but operated on a clean slate majority principle, and 40-year-old electoral boundaries were retained—and Sri Lanka, where disenfranchised Tamils are used for delimitation purposes as 'population' to confer an additional 14 seats on Sinhalese voters). There are systems dependent on units which favour particular groups (Georgia, USA, until 1963), on loading of particular constituencies where there are concentrations of minority group voters (Rhodesia), or on the application of weighting criteria in delimitation to give proportionately more rural than urban constituencies (Malaysia—where more Malays are rural and more Chinese urban, and South Africa where English voters concentrate in towns). There may also be biased administration of elections and failure by authorities to take corrective action (USA until 1966, and Nigeria before 1966).

Much more drastic than these manipulative methods is the authorisation by law of population transfer of minority communities to areas where they are not regarded as a political threat (Russia between 1941 and 1944 and South Africa under its *apartheid* laws).

A more sophisticated approach, but which equally effectively denies all political rights (and many economic rights which are not accorded to aliens) is the enactment of restrictive citizenship laws. This technique has been applied to the Tamils of Indian origin in Sri Lanka where the effect was that by 1952, on a constitution envisaging that Tamils would hold 29 of the 95 parliamentary seats, they in fact held only 12. Similar policies have been applied to Chinese in the Philippines and in Indonesia, and to Asians and other non-Africans in Malawi, Kenya, Zanzibar and Uganda.

The economic sphere The legal mechanisms designed to secure economic advantages for one ethnic group as opposed to another are the same irrespective of the motivation for their enactment. They may of course be designed to perpetuate the economic power of one group (South Africa and Rhodesia) or they may be designed to remedy what is seen by the dominant elite as imbalance in patterns of economic power as between the power positions of the various groups. Such imbalance may have occurred in respect of a minority community which has a disproportionately low share of national wealth and has had economic opportunities denied to it (as in the USA), or it may occur in respect of a minority community which has acquired a disproportionately powerful place in the economy, because of its relationship with a colonial power (the East African Asians used by the British for middle range public service and public works; and the Indian Tamils, brought to Ceylon in the nineteenth century as indentured labourers), or because of its active economic orientation (East African Asians; Chinese in Malaysia, the Philippines and Indonesia; and Tamils in Ceylon) or its much more rapid modernisation (the Tamils responded more actively to mission education and to urbanisation in Ceylon).

Whether laws and administrative action designed to remedy such imbalances are described as 'affirmative action' or 'reverse discrimination', or as 'national development' or 'discrimination', will depend upon whether the commentator is a beneficiary of the laws or not. If the emphasis is on remedying disadvantage and lack of opportunity (such as special educational programmes, special technical assistance programmes, special loan programmes for help in setting up co-operatives) or is protective (protection of native land against sale to capitalist entrepreneurs) it can be more readily tolerated by non-recipients. If it becomes an instrument of economic attack on other communities by denial of the right to engage in their traditional occupations then it is proper to describe the technique as one of domination. In contrast, if the economic advantages are a 'plus' in the system, an increment, rather than something already in existence being transferred from one group to another in a zero-sum game then it would be unfair to describe the new laws as primarily being oriented to domination. However, although non-zero sum transfers are less open to criticism, even those involve departure from the equality of access principle from the standpoint of an individual denied access to the newly available resources, e.g. the Tamil denied a place in a new Sinhalese medical faculty.

The best known economic advantages provided by law are restrictions on land ownership and occupation. Many have been protective of colonised indigenous groups (as in New Zealand, South Africa, Rhodesia, Canada and the USA). Others have been designed to perpetuate the economic power of European settlers by grossly unequal land division (Rhodesia and South Africa). In some developing countries previously unsettled rural land has been opened up by establishing new irrigation projects, co-operatives and marketing schemes for the dominant group only (Malaysia; Sri Lanka). In others, large land areas are reserved for indigenous groups as opposed to persons of settler descent (in Fiji, Indians are over half the population, but owned only 1·7 per cent of the land in Fiji where the Fijian 42·3 per cent of the population had reserved for it 83·8 per cent of the land). Another technique is to prohibit aliens from owning land and to define aliens so as to exclude persons not of indigenous descent (in the Philippines many second and third generation Chinese are thus excluded).

Another technique for changing the economic structure is frequently employed where a minority group has hitherto monopolised the roles of middleman in trade or of small scale industrialist. Administrative discretion to refuse or grant trading and business licences and import or export permits is used on racial grounds or on grounds of non-citizenship (East African states, Indonesia and Malaysia). Obviously such policies may in part be evaded by 'buying' a tame nominee.

Government contracts have been used in two ways. They have been used directly to give benefits to a particular ethnic group (in Malaysia small public works contracts are preferentially awarded to Malay contractors). They have been used indirectly to require contractors to employ a fixed percentage of ethnic group members and to introduce training and promotion schemes for such employees (in the United States the construction industry has been forced to take on black employees and to give them proper training).

Control of employment in the Civil Service or in government controlled public corporations is another means of ensuring that employment patterns conform to the aims of the dominant group. In Malaysia, Malays are guaranteed that appointments will be on the basis of four Malays for every non-Malay. In Sri Lanka, whereas at independence about 30 per cent of government service admissions were Tamils today the percentage is down to around 6 per cent.

Economic nationalism throughout the world has resulted in policies stipulating that work permits are required before any alien can be employed. Such a policy is justifiable to protect the inhabitants of the state against unemployment and unfair competition from migrant workers willing to accept lower wages and a lower standard of living. United Kingdom governments have argued that their purpose in cutting down the flow of 'coloured' Commonwealth immigrants by the Acts of 1962 and 1968 was to improve relations, which would otherwise be endangered by social and economic problems consequent on the influx. Similar arguments have been put forward by other European states faced by an influx of immigrant workers (Switzerland). The position of the United Kingdom is complicated by the fact that Indian and Chinese communities, transported to or encouraged to go to various parts of the Empire for economic reasons, chose to remain citizens of the United Kingdom and colonies and to elect not to accept citizenship from newly independent African and Asian states, rightly fearing that in the long run they would face economic discrimination. Not very different in degree has been the attitude of economic nationalism adopted by African states such as Tanzania, Kenya and Uganda, and by the Philippines and Indonesia to persons of foreign descent already settled in such countries. Governments have sought by a combination of nationality laws and the requirement of work permits for aliens to 'Africanise' or to 'de-Sinicise'.

The power of private employers to discriminate has in most states been permissible in terms of the law of contract and is widespread in countries with majority/minority ethnic and religious divisions. If law does not prohibit, it authorises. In the United States and in the United Kingdom such discrimination (subject to very limited exceptions) is unlawful, and a variety of mechanisms, both conciliatory and adversary, have been set up to prevent discrimination. In the United Kingdom, except in Northern Ireland, religious discrimination affecting private employment is unregulated: in 1976 legislation was enacted for Northern Ireland establishing a Fair Employment Commission. Only in the United States is 'affirmative' action to remedy past imbalances of recruitment and promotion permissible. In the United Kingdom (apart from exemptions in regard to special needs in training, education or welfare), reverse discrimination remains unlawful.

Perhaps equally important in determining employment patterns are trade union rules and practices about membership and provision of union facilities, especially representation. If unions discriminate, minority groups are likely to be denied vocational employment opportunities because many employers prefer unionised labour as they then have to deal only with union representatives. In the United Kingdom since 1968, racial discrimination by unions has been unlawful, while the same results have been achieved in the United States by judicial development of the 'equal protection' doctrine combined with statute.

Fiscal policies are also used to further the interests of particular ethnic groups. In Malaysia, Sri Lanka, Kenya and Tanzania state monies have been directed to development projects and grants for only one ethnic group and its members. This is seen as correcting imbalanced patterns of economic predominance by particular groups in the agricultural or industrial sectors and as helping those who have been denied economic advance. Similar policy issues have arisen in European states where economic policies and the growth of state industry are seen as favouring particular ethnic groups concentrated in the region where public investment is made (Belgium, France, the United Kingdom).

The best known instruments of economic nationalism are nationalisation policies directed against non-citizens. In socialist states following a general policy of nationalisation and where there are coincidentally wealthy ethnic communities, the impact of such policies will be more severe on such communities. Thus in Tanzania the nationalisation policy in regard to export-import business, wholesale trade, industrial production, transport, retail distribution and landlordism led to the transfer of economic enterprise into the hands of an African government from an Asian business community, and to an exodus of that community. Similar effects can be achieved by direct taxation policies which hit at economically dominant entrepreneurial communities (such as Indians and Chinese). Conversely, indirect taxation policies will shift economic burdens to the group who usually are part of a disadvantaged ethnic community (Rhodesia, where indirect taxation brings Africans into the tax net).

The cultural sphere To discover whether cultural laws are used to secure domination would require study of the administrative practices of particular states. There is often variance between the legal provisions and the practice, which may be tolerant and accommodating. Furthermore laws in this area are differently perceived from different viewpoints: what is described by a minority as forced assimilation is seen by the majority as preservation of national identity. Language, schooling and cultural habits and traditions can be explosive issues in polyethnic states.

Various possibilities are open in respect of official language policy. These may be one language only; there may be multiple languages on an equal basis; and there may be a hierarchy of preferred languages. In federal and pre-federal states the situation may be complicated by different official languages at the federal and at the regional level. The significance of official languages is that it is usually necessary to speak that language to advance economically. Consequently, parents from other linguistic groups tend to educate their children in official language schools, thereby in the long run downgrading the significance of their own language. (It is this factor which has led to Quebec's recent specification of French not only as official language but as required language for the education of all children, other than those who have a parent or a sibling educated at an English language school in Quebec, and as a required language for businesses over a specified size.)

Adoption of a single official language is a policy seen as domination by minority linguistic groups (as in Malaysia, Burma, Thailand, Iran, Sri Lanka, and in the United Kingdom until the Welsh Language Act 1967 made provision for greater use of Welsh). The proposed introduction of Hindi as the sole official language of India led to serious political differences until a compromise was reached in 1967. Similar political strife has arisen in various Canadian provinces and in Quebec over French language policies. Again in Belgium there have been ethno-linguistic disputes for the time damped down by new constitutional arrangements envisaging pre-federal arrangements based on language regions. Specification of use of the majority language only is likely to be particularly contentious in the context of the conduct of government business, including letter writing, or in the context of requirements that civil servants pass language examinations, or in the context of a particular language only being specified for use in the courts, or if a particular language is specified as the medium of school instruction. All these are grievances of the Tamil minority in Sri Lanka. Another context in which single official language use, or, conversely, limited use of a minority group language, is seen as designed to weaken the minority's cultural inheritance is that of language use on national radio and television networks. Unless minority languages are used by the media their proponents fear that they will not remain living languages. Language used in public places may also be regarded as symbolically significant: this is the case in connection with demands for road traffic signs and public notices to be in a minority language (as demanded in Wales).

In polyethnic countries there are many aspects of and issues in education which can become the focus for intense antagonism. There are major questions to be decided. Should there be a monopoly of state education, or should voluntary schools be permitted to continue in existence; be permitted to increase in numbers; or have their educational programmes carefully directed by the state? If there are voluntary schools, should these receive financial support; if so, how much; and should they be permitted to charge fees?

By the way in which an education system answers these questions can it be judged. Sri Lanka is an example of a country applying domination techniques in education. Northern Ireland,

Holland and Belgium, with separate voluntary schools state-funded, are all countries where the state education authorities have compromised and implemented policies countenancing pluralism.

In the sphere of cultural habits and traditions there are contexts which give rise to perceptions by minority groups that they are being dominated. National holidays, the national flag, and national dress may reflect only the traditions of the majority group. In the context of religious observance denial by law of freedom to conduct rituals, to observe dietary rules and to observe religious holiday requirements will be seen as weakening the cultural traditions of minority groups. In the present century, with increasing state funding as the major source of support for cultural activities, if adequate state funds are not made available for minority groups' cultural activities and for public facilities for communicating knowledge of the groups' histories and cultural traditions (through museums and libraries) the culture of the groups will be more easily displaced by other elements in the national culture and which are more frequently put before group members in the form of entertainment or educational activity.

Even more significant in the transmission and maintenance of group cultures is access to the public opinion process. Crucial to the ability of minorities to perpetuate their cultural or ideological identity are the traditional civil liberties of freedom of expression and association. This is even more significant with the rise of literacy and the growth of newspaper circulation, and with the technological developments of radio and television with its powerful direct and immediate impact. Important issues are to what extent does a minority group have access to the media to put across its point of view? What controls are there on freedom of expression? Such controls may be negative, preventing the group from furthering its ideology, or positive, protecting the group from the stirring up of feelings of racial or religious hatred. Is there freedom of association, both by means of ability to establish a political party to articulate minority demands, and in the form of trade unions primarily identified with one minority group?

In Sri Lanka, in Malaysia and in African one-party states not all these questions can be answered to the satisfaction of minority groups. In some instances the denial of facilities for communication can be ascribed to a wish to integrate and to remove sensitive issues from public debate, but in other cases it is occasioned by a wish to impose the ideology of the dominant group.

The sphere of public order and lawful force In the last resort political and legal systems are maintained by force or the threat of force. That force is, in a modern state, bound down by rules as to how it is organised, when it may be used and when others may use countervailing force. Also significant in this context as governing situations which are a prelude to the eruption of force is public order law. Those who seek to maintain the current order use legal rules governing public processions, meetings, sit-ins and trespass, unlawful assemblies, obstruction of the highway, public nuisance, conspiracy, seditious speech-making and literature, preventive detention and the whole panoply of 'offences against the state' to keep protest within bounds determined by the judicial machinery and by legislative provision. Both statutes and judicial precedents are subject to change whenever it appears to the power holders in a society that protest may threaten the current order. In such circumstances traditional civil and political liberties are relegated and coercive public order law will be used or will be changed to facilitate continued domination by the current power holders.

The notion of 'institutionalised violence' is not easily accepted by the average citizen who has been socialised into accepting the legitimacy of law and the legal system. Generally he does not perceive either public order law or the public agents of law enforcement as manifestations of the power of the dominant group. If the aim of those in control is to seek an integrated and stable society, the last thing they will wish is that the law enforcement agents of the state (and here the reference is to the police and in exceptional cases the armed forces) be seen as the tools of one group. It is therefore not only because rulers are aware of possible abuses by law enforcement officers, but also because the acceptability of the regime to minorities and the likelihood of peace in society will be influenced by the degree to which minorities perceive themselves as being 'oppressed' by state officials, that rulers take action to ensure that police forces behave with propriety.[3] The awareness of the wisdom of such an approach began in the United States with attempts to recruit and promote black policemen and then extended into areas of professional training, of teaching proper behaviour under circumstances of provocation, of techniques for maintaining good community relations, of the necessity for establishing a police community relations section, of giving the minority some participation or say in the control of the police force, of providing grievance machinery for complaints about police behaviour backed by adequate disciplinary machinery, of establishing codes governing police discretion, and of ensuring independent and even-handed prosecution of offences. These techniques have been imported into Northern Ireland since 1969 and have gradually begun to affect Catholics' perceptions of the behaviour of the Royal Ulster Constabulary. Obviously politically-aware members of any minority realise that in the last resort the police are upholders of the existing political order. (The sociologically sophisticated will speak of 'repressive tolerance'.) Nonetheless hostility can be moderated by adoption of such techniques and better group relations maintained. Awareness of this is also influencing English police forces in their dealings with immigrant communities.

Everything said about public perceptions of the behaviour of the police force applies with equal emphasis to the armed forces. Obviously in a deeply divided society a strong government force and security laws are required to maintain intercommunal peace and to provide the framework within which compromise can operate. In such societies suspicions that communal differences are being reflected in the armed forces' recruitment and promotion policies may well stimulate military coups engineered by another communal group (Sudan and Pakistan). In fact, the army can be used as an integrating mechanism by educating soldiers and acculturating them in an integrated force (Israel and India).

PLURALIST TECHNIQUES

In a plural society separate institutions are provided for different ethnic groups. Pluralist policies range along a scale of degrees of 'separateness'. Groups will share some common and compulsory institutions e.g. the courts, but will be accorded different exclusive institutions in other spheres e.g. separate representation in a legislature. Usually the aim is to recognise the special and peculiar interests of the minority. Thus positive rights in the cultural sphere may be recognised e.g. language rights, protection of communal schools or distinctive rules of family law. Occasionally the minority institutions may be tokenism, with the real aim being to keep the minority in an inferior position with politically impotent segregated institutions e.g. reserved racial representation in South Africa. In contrast, in a tolerant plural society, where there is a desire to accord full participation as well as protection to the minority, there are often not only formal plural institutions and arrangements effectively but informally securing pluralism, but also conventional political practices which are plural in character e.g. conventions in Switzerland and Canada as to the ethno-linguistic composition of the cabinet.

GROUP AUTONOMY ON TERRITORIAL PRINCIPLES

Constitutions have been classified in terms of the balance between centralising and decentralising forces as manifested in the state structure. If the powers of government are organised under a single central authority, while whatever powers possessed by local units are held at the sufferance of the central government, which can exercise supreme legislative authority, the constitution is described as unitary. If the powers of government are distributed between central and local government and the central authority is limited by the powers secured to the territorial units, the state is federal. In Dicey's words the 'federal state is a political contrivance intended to reconcile national unity and power with the maintenance of state rights'.[4]

There is a spectrum of federal societies varying according to the relative strength of the demands for unity and territorial diversity. There may be little practical difference between federal states with unitary tendencies and unitary states with massive devolution: the essential nature of federalism is to be sought for, not in the shadings of legal and constitutional terminology, but in the forces—economic, social, political, cultural—that have made the outward forms of federalism.[5] Indeed administrative devolution can provide an alternative to a technically federal state.

Federalism

The factors distinguishing federations from decentralised unitary states are: a retention of some sovereignty both in the units and the central unit; the fact that units and centre are in some respects co-ordinate and not subordinate to each other; the fact that some fields are within the exclusive competence of the units and some of the centre; and a constitutional guarantee of autonomy ensuring relative permanence to the existence of centre and units. The federal principle of constitutional organisation is designed to allow integrative and divisive forces to operate simultaneously: with two levels of government in each unit and operating upon each citizen the central government wields the unifying forces, while the separate local (provincial, central, state) governments in territorial regions provide the diversity. In such a system units and centre are committed to working together and to compromising in a common framework rather than to disagreeing and fragmenting. The differing groups can make their views known and have a say in decision making, facilitated by channels for communication and for compromise. A federation is not a fixed and immutable framework: it is subject to change and development, both formal and informal (co-operative federalism as in Canada). Just as the federal superstructure affects social and political attitudes, so conversely these forces interact with federal political institutions. However, if political attitudes (e.g. in an authoritarian one-party state such as the USSR) are such that centre and units operate as one under the direction of the centre with the understanding that at all times the centre's wishes will prevail, then, although the state is federal in law, it is functionally unitary. Obviously a federal constitution does not in itself ensure that there will be genuine federalism, or toleration of real diversity amongst the units.

The prognosis for successful federalism depends upon the circumstances under which the federal state has been created. If it is merely a legacy of imperialism and it is a vast territory with agglomerations of ethnic groupings, then the state will face almost insuperable difficulties, which would have arisen irrespective of its principle of constitutional organisation. 'Federation' will have been adopted as a last resort and as giving the best chance to the new state of surviving intact. Many new federations failed: it is surprising that more have not collapsed. British advisers treated federal government as providing a panacea both for the communal problems of the emerging independent states and for the imperial purpose of maintaining the integrity of their former colonial possessions. The histories of two European federations, created after the Second World War in nation states which came into existence after the First World War on the dissolution of the Austro-Hungarian monarchy, have also been chequered. They have faced constant tendencies to fragmentation, several times making major amendments to their federal arrangements (Yugoslavia and Czechoslavakia).

Only if a federation has arisen out of organic growth, supported by a need for common defence and a desire to exploit economic opportunities, has it in the long run been successful e.g. Switzerland, United States, Australia. Mere artificial creations are unlikely to be held together by constitutional glue and in the long run to survive basic disunity. Even generous constitutional arrangements do not create unity where there are competing cultures. Thus after a century of federation in which French Canadian culture has been protected by dual language rights, by provincial control of education, by recognition for the Roman Catholic church, and by virtually complete autonomy for Quebec— including some *de facto* international representation on Dominion missions and power to influence the political balance within Canada many French Canadians today demand secession from Canada and an independent state of Quebec. They see themselves as being economically discriminated against and colonised by English-speaking businessmen and settlers, with federal power a brake on their own development. In reality French Canadian cultural patterns have led to French Canadians' relative inability to meet the demands of an industrial economy.

Is it possible to discern issues occasioning conflict in polyethnic federations and can institutional arrangements reduce the likelihood of conflict?

(i) Linguism has been a constant cause of conflict: whether in respect of the official language (India and Pakistan); or in respect of education policy (Quebec); or in respect of state geographical boundaries (India). To meet these problems a 'bargaining' approach, flexibility, responsiveness and a willingness to accommodate by the federal authorities are prerequisites.[6] So is a certain amount of forethought in establishing institutional mechanisms *before* any conflict arises. The following arrangements help if the region is homogeneous (if it is heterogeneous there are majority/minority problems in the region itself—India, Pakistan and Nigeria).

1. All major languages to be equal on the federal level, with self-determination as to each region's official language combined with a policy of providing facilities for large minority groups within regions;

2. The media of educational instruction to be regionally agreed;

3. An independent regional boundary commission to be established and to be charged with reporting every five years and recommending adjustments in the light of demographic, linguistic and ethnic factors. With such a regular process linguistic tensions in India between 1950 and 1956 might have been minimised. Linguistic loyalties are there: they will not disappear by refusing to recognise them. A similar approach led to proposals to create a new canton of Jura. If amendment of the Swiss Constitution is approved in a referendum to be held in September 1978, the conditions under which Jurassien separatism has become a political force in Switzerland will be weakened.

(ii) Fiscal disputes over allocation of funds between regions and between regions and centre, especially for development purposes, have been frequent. Federal economic policies are seen as favouring one ethnic group to the disadvantage of others (Yugoslavia is alleged to advance Serbian interests). Some devices to preclude such dissension have been utilised. They are:

1. An independent Fiscal Commission to examine the allocation of revenues as between centre and states, and reporting every three years to facilitate regular adjustment;

2. Intergovernmental councils and organisations consulting on economic planning and policies;

3. Inter-delegation of power in advance so that a state government can act for the federal government or vice versa. Swiss taxes and social security are cantonally administered by authorities felt to be closer and more congenial to local populations.

(iii) Fears of domination by a large ethnic state within a federation have caused instability (in Nigeria Northern domination was feared; in India populous Hindi states are feared by Dravidian states; and in Yugoslavia Serb dominance is feared). Constitutional changes on the following lines have helped meet such fears:

1. Restructuring of the federation by dividing existing states into a larger number of units (Nigeria—where it has so far been most successful). This approach also mitigates the problem of minorities within a minority which controls a region: they can now have their own regions.

2. Enhancement of the units at the expense of the centre (Yugoslavia in 1968);

3. Provision of a constitutional veto by groups of regional representatives, which veto then brings into operation a referendum procedure (Yugoslavia);

4. Limitation of the scope of emergency powers accorded the central government so that it cannot take over the functions of state government.

Regionalism or devolution

Similar to federalism in distributing power territorially, is the principle of regionalism or devolution. Here a unitary state provides for the delegation of executive and legislative governmental powers to a locally elected body. It differs from federalism in that a devolved legislature and administration are not independent of the central legislature, while the central body can override the regional body's decisions by legislation, and sometimes even by administrative veto. Nor does the region enjoy the same degree of financial autonomy as a federal territory. However, depending upon the degree of supervision in practice and its freedom once revenues have been allocated to it, a devolved administration may determine its spending priorities as freely as a state in a federation.

Northern Ireland between 1922 and 1972 had a devolved parliament and executive responsible for most governmental powers other than income tax, defence, and foreign affairs. For 50 years the majority community, the Protestants, exclusively exercised political power and, until 1969, did so with little regard to the Roman Catholic nationalist minority, which favoured union with the Republic of Ireland. By 1972 it was apparent that in a politically and religiously deeply divided society there could only be government by consent of both communities—a consent not forthcoming. Devolution was then ended by the United Kingdom Parliament. From January to May 1974 there was another experiment in devolution but this time without law and order powers which had been the subject of inter-community disputes. The new Northern Ireland Assembly and a 'power-sharing' Executive collapsed after widespread industrial action by Protestants making it clear that they rejected such arrangements. Subsequent attempts to get local politicians to agree to new constitutional arrangements have failed. Northern Ireland is in 1978 under 'direct rule', without a local legislature, and governed by a Secretary of State for Northern Ireland exercising executive and legislative powers which the Assembly and Executive would otherwise have enjoyed.

The Italian Constitution has adopted the principle of regionalism. Italy is divided into regions, provinces and communes. Five special autonomous regions have extensive powers either because of communal problems (Trentino-Alto Adige (the South Tyrol) with its large German-speaking minority seeking reunification with the Austrian Tyrol),[7] or because of contiguity to neighbouring states (Friuli-Venezia Giulia which includes Trieste and abuts Yugoslavia and Valle d'Aosta adjacent to France), or because of geographical separation from Italy and local desire for autonomy (Sicily and Sardinia). Regions have regional councils, an executive *giunta* with a president, taxing powers, a share in national taxes, financial autonomy, powers of control over urban and local police, roads, regional transport, town planning, local government, agriculture and industry. Most interesting from the point of view of possible arrangements for minority problems is the Trentino-Alto Adige region and its province of Bolzano. Since 1972 a revised autonomy statute has conferred a considerable degree of local power on Bolzano, where German speakers are in a majority. This flowed from a 'pact' in 1969 between Italian and Austrian governments and South Tyrolean politicians to protect both German and Italian communities in the region and province and to accord autonomy and equality to the German-dominated province. The new arrangements to deal with the South Tyrol question were brought about partly by international pressure, partly by terrorism and partly through willingness by the Italian Government to make concessions and to compromise. Many of the devices to satisfy minorities with political claims were used. In the region, German became an official language enjoying equality with Italian. Education became less controversial, coming for the most part under local control. Fiscal arrangements (the regional and provincial budgets) were to be agreed by both linguistic groups and mutual vetoes of sorts were given. Proportional representation is used to elect both provincial and regional legislatures. Proportional representation also applies in the administration, so that approximately one third of the members of the regional government are German speakers and one third

Italian speakers. In the provincial government two thirds are German speakers and one third Italian. The German and Italian parties also operate *de facto* coalitions. Proportionate access to the civil service of province and region is already observed and ultimately the same principle is to be applied to Italian state posts in the region. Finally, the Austrian Government has agreed to declare the South Tyrol question closed after finalisation of the constitutional changes implementing the 1969 package of agreed measures to deal with the political problem of the German minority in Trentino-Alto Adige.

The constitutional changes in Belgium in 1970, dividing Belgium into three regions, with the subsequent creation of consultative regional institutions in August 1974, is another example of dealing with majority problems by constitutional amendment, legislation and compromise. The regional organs will operate in the general political, economic and cultural fields and there will be re-distribution of power as between the Houses of Parliament and the King and his ministers and regional institutions.

South African regionalism in the form of semi-autonomous Bantustans, supervised by a central government representative, dependent on grants in aid from the South African Parliament and subject to its concurrent legislative power, show that it is not the form of institutions, but the realities of economic power and political relationships, which are the determinants of whether there is meaningful regional autonomy: just as there is federalism in Russia so long as the central authorities do not object, so there is regionalism in South Africa. Independent Bantustans, such as the Transkei, are on a different basis, but they are still dependent on South Africa subventions.

Administrative decentralisation

An alternative to creating local organs endowed with power is a policy of decentralising national administration. A regional office staffed by national civil servants with power to implement distinctive regional policies is established. Such a regional administrative office has a large hierarchy of civil servants headed by a cabinet minister, who can, by his influence in the cabinet, secure the adoption of distinctive regional policies. Additionally, there may be localised administration by state departments who maintain regional organisations and offices; sometimes overall control of these is delegated to the regional office. Additionally some specialisation occurs in national legislative institutions with specialised groups of legislators scrutinising the activities of the regional administration and those of any other national civil servants operating in the region. Such a policy has been adopted in respect of Scotland since 1885. The Secretary of State for Scotland heads the Scottish Office in Edinburgh and also has functions in relation to administrative arrangements of several United Kingdom departments operating in Scotland. The Scottish Office's main powers to administer regionally relate to education, home affairs (police and law and order), health, and agriculture and fisheries. Scotland also has its own legal and judicial system for which the Scottish Lord Advocate is responsible. Parliamentary institutions in the form of the Scottish Grand Committee, the Scottish Standing Committee and the Select Committee for Scottish Affairs exercise effective control over legislation for Scotland. Scottish nationalism has now resulted in demands for retransfer of legislative and executive autonomy to Scotland and an ending of the Union. Currently the United Kingdom Parliament has under consideration the Scotland Bill, which seeks to mollify and mitigate nationalist feelings by introducing a devolution pattern very similar to that in Northern Ireland from 1922 to 1972.

Local government

In all communal situations the difficulties, which exist even in a relatively homogeneous society, of striking a balance between democracy and local feelings on the one side, and efficiency and national interests on the other, are exacerbated. In a communally divided society local government becomes an intensely divisive issue, particularly where the communities are interdispersed. In Northern Ireland (arising from historical accidents but until 1969 deliberately left unreformed) a multiplicity of urban and rural district councils and of county and county borough councils allowed one community to dominate the other, especially in housing and employment policies. The deep communal divisions in conjunction with dispersed communities and small local government units seemed to result in domination rather than in pluralistic co-operation. The approach then followed was centralisation. Under United Kingdom government pressure local government was restructured to remove some major functions to the Parliament of the province and to transfer other controversial functions, such as housing, to a central housing authority.

Another approach is to redraw boundaries along communal lines and to accord each community control in its own area. This was done by the Cyprus Constitution of 1960, but was unacceptable to the Makarios Government, who proposed constitutional amendments to merge the municipalities. These proposals, with others, led to the breakdown of the 1960 constitutional arrangements.

Community development authorities

In some developing countries it is thought that economic development through enhanced agricultural productivity will result from attitudes developed in local government institutions. Where there are relatively backward tribal communities mixed in with more enterprising communities, another objective of setting up community development institutions has been the strengthening of feelings of group identity to assist local ethnic communities to preserve themselves against tendencies to disintegration in a modernising society. Thus in India the *panchayati raj* system of local councils provides for tribally composed councils possessing executive, legislative and judicial power in the tribal area. Participation, economic development, and preservation of tribal identity are all aims of the system.

ELECTORAL LAWS AND COMPOSITION OF THE LEGISLATURE

Group divisions may be formally recognised, either by establishing separate voter's qualifications and communal voters' rolls for each group, or by establishing specially designated seats for each group whether or not proportionate to the size of the group in relation to other groups. The principle of proportionality, implemented by proportional representation voting systems, or the provision of bicameral legislatures with a regionally composed upper house, are methods of informally ensuring that minority groups are represented. Such methods may be used in combination (Fiji and Lebanon, where both formal and informal techniques exist).

The demand for communal institutions is occasioned by fear of domination by other communities, particularly marked where there is a majoritarian approach by the dominant community. Communal electoral systems are significant not only because they determine the composition of the legislature and thence affect the likelihood of constitutional change, but also because they determine the composition of the government, unless there is a presidential system.

The danger of formal communalism is that it encourages political patterns reinforcing ethnic lines and cuts down the occasions for communal interaction among the ordinary voting members of the community. The effect on the elites is not so marked, but, even in their case, vested interest in respect of their own power and their relationship with their own community tend to cause a reluctance to compromise or to act counter to communal loyalties as currently perceived.

The variants of communal representation are set out below:

Separate electoral rolls and separate blocs of seats Separate electoral rolls are maintained. (If there is a qualitative franchise instead of merely referring to racial criteria, the communal character may be obscured so as to avoid any charges of 'racialism'.) The voters on each electoral roll vote for communal candidates occupying separate blocs of seats. (This system applied in Cyprus under the 1960 Constitution (there were 35 Greek Cypriots: 15 Turkish Cypriots), in New Zealand (76 ordinary seats for non-Maoris and 4 seats for Maoris since 1867) and in India (15 per cent of the seats are reserved until 1985 for the Scheduled Tribes and Scheduled Castes effectively giving the Untouchables 77 out of 522 seats).) It has also been applied in Fiji, Rhodesia and South Africa.)

Separate electoral rolls, separate blocs of seats and cross voting Separate voters' qualifactions, dressed up in a qualitative franchise so as not to appear racialistic, may be used in combination with a cross voting system. Each roll has its own seats, but voters may also cross vote, and cross votes will then be adjusted to count as a fixed percentage of the votes cast. The purpose of cross voting is to ensure a minimal degree of support for candidates from each community. This system applied in Southern Rhodesia from 1962 to 1969. In Northern Rhodesia, between 1962 and the grant of the Zambian Constitution of 1964, a similar system, but also requiring a candidate to reach a certain percentage of votes from each community, resulted in failure to fill seats. Such systems give difficulty not only because there must be minimal cross-community support, but because there are problems of definition (what is a 'community'?). Such a system, if there is not to be a qualitative franchise, makes communal rolls or party registration as an identifying factor, a pre-condition. Cross voting has been proposed for Northern Ireland.

Communal seats in fixed proportions, but with common voting In this system there are a fixed number of national seats for each community e.g. in Fiji 19 national seats for Fijians, 10 for Indians and 5 for others. Members for these seats are elected by all voters irrespective of the roll on which they are registered. Again the purpose is to ensure a minimum degree of support from voters of other communities.

Proportional representation systems The arguments in favour of proportional representation (PR) are based on fair shares, the right of minority groups to be heard, the prevention of large electoral swings entirely removing minority representation, the right of voters that their votes should count fully and not be wasted, the fact that it gives individual voters more freedom of choice, that it allows flexibility and crossing of party lines, that it encourages coalition-type governments in which each party has to compromise with other parties thus tending to the emergence of a centre grouping, and that it encourages parties to have regard to the interests of voters other than their own supporters so as to secure later preferences votes. In contrast objections of complexity and cost are relatively insignificant. The system has some difficulty in dealing with by-elections, but the major objections, that it results in multiplicity of parties and instability of government, can, paradoxically, be used in its favour, in situations where, as in Northern Ireland, the problem is that for 50 years one party has had the monopoly of power.

There are many variations on PR. In the list systems control of candidate selection is entirely in the hands of the political parties uninfluenced by voter choice, the top candidates nominated by the parties being elected. Seats are filled from party lists of preferred candidates in such a way that the seats filled by that party in proportion to the total number of seats is the same as the proportion between the votes cast for that party and the total number of votes cast. Methods of calculating the quota which will secure a candidate election, result in other variations. The larger the constituencies, with greater numbers of seats, the more proportional will be the results. Multi-member constituencies with two or three members are unlikely to result in representation for many minorities. Of the various systems the single transferable vote system, employed in Ireland and in Northern Ireland since 1973, has the advantage over the list system of allowing individual preferences as between candidates. Arguably the adoption of PR in Holland and in Belgium has been a factor in keeping communally mixed states together. PR may also be used in a bicameral system for selection of upper house members, as in India.

The alternative vote The alternative vote system is not a PR system although it is often described as one. The system allows voters in single member constituencies to list their preferences, and the first candidate who obtains an absolute majority of votes, generally after elimination of less popular candidates and transfer of their preferences, is elected. The system results in election of the least unpopular candidate and leads to bargaining and electoral pacts. The system was adopted in Southern Rhodesia to preclude the election of African candidates if European votes were split at first count. In practice it resulted in 'middle of the road' European candidates obtaining African votes, thereby tending to keep Rhodesian Front 'right wingers' out, even though they might poll the largest number of votes. Had African voters exercised the alternative vote in the 1962 elections, as they did in 1958, the Rhodesian Front would not have come to power. The alternative vote was abolished in 1964 by a Rhodesian Front controlled parliament.

Proportional representation with the single ballot system and communal representation in a single electoral college This system has been employed in the Lebanon since the National Pact 1943. The entire electorate in any constituency votes for candidates for all the various communally designated seats i.e. for one Maronite, one Sunni Muslim, one Greek Orthodox and one Druze candidate in the constituency. The numbers of communal seats for each confessional community are calculated on a formula of six Christians to five non-Christians based on the 1932 census. In practice voters rarely split their lists, and consequently candidates in each sect attempted to link themselves with popular candidates in another sect. A ticket (list) would be elected, thus aligning leaders from different sects together as against others in their own sect. Although interconfessional coalitions tended to result, ideological alliances did not follow, and no coherent policies were developed. What occurred was a process of opportunistic bargaining, candidates remaining communally orientated, factional and veto conscious, looking over their shoulders at their own community, and representing themselves as guardians of their own communities.

Bicameral systems with communal representation Communal representation may be carried over into the upper house. Upper houses are less significant where legislation is concerned, usually merely having delaying powers, but their composition is important for constitutional amendment procedures. Communal representation can be found in Fiji.

Regional representatives in federal bicameral systems Here there is informal pluralism in that communal factors are not the criterion of representation. Instead, regions of the federation are represented, usually on a basis of equality as between regions, in contrast with the lower house where population numbers are the principle of allocation of seats to regions. Examples of federal plural states with regional representation are India with its House of the People, Malaysia with its Senate, and quinticameral Yugoslavia with its Chamber of Nationalities.

Special communal legislative bodies A remarkable feature of the Cyprus Constitution of 1960 was the provision in Article 86 for two Communal Chambers, each elected by the relevant Turkish or Greek community, and having exclusive legislative competence in fields likely to occasion controversy between the groups and relating to group cultural identity, for example in all educational, teaching and cultural, religious matters and matters of personal status.

Group veto powers Communal representation in the legislature is usually related to modes of constitutional amendment by the requirement of a weighted majority, such as two-thirds of the total membership of a legislative body or even of a three-quarters majority (Fiji). In some cases there are explicit communal vetoes—as where approval by a majority of the group representatives or in a separate group referendum is required (Southern Rhodesia between 1961 and 1965). In Cyprus separate simple majorities of both Greek and Turkish representatives were even required for some ordinary legislation such as laws modifying the Electoral Law, imposing duties and taxes, or relating to the municipalities.

PARTICIPATION IN EXECUTIVE GOVERNMENT

Special patterns of executive government can be found in plural countries. These may have been imposed by an imperial power (Northern Ireland), agreed as a compromise (Lebanon, Cyprus and South Tyrol) or resulted from organic development (Switzerland).

Formal power sharing Constitutional provisions may require the communities to work together as a coalition. The Cyprus Constitution 1960 provided that there was to be a fixed 7:3 ratio as between Greek and Turkish Ministers (who would have been elected on separate communal rolls), and either the ministry of foreign affairs, defence or security had to be given to a Turk. All Council of Ministers decisions had to be taken by an absolute majority, and any decision concerning foreign affairs, defence or security was subject to veto either by the Greek President or the Turkish Vice-President. Such complicated communal arrangements, even in the most amicable of atmospheres, ran the risk of unworkability: with Greek and Turkish intransigence they broke down in four years. The Greeks wanted majoritarianism and the Turks wanted an over-generous calculation of communal proportionality as the principle of constitutional arrangement.

Power sharing was equally unsuccessful in Northern Ireland when introduced in 1974. After proportional representation elections on the transferable vote, the Secretary of State for Northern Ireland appointed a power sharing Executive with both Protestant and Catholic members coming from several political parties and effectively commanding a majority in the new Assembly. Consultative parliamentary Committees to advise on departmental policies were also appointed and in each case chaired by the relevant head of department, while the membership of the committees as a whole reflected the balance of parties in the Assembly. By early 1974 the bulk of the Protestant community had withdrawn its support from the Executive, and, after large scale industrial action against the Executive in May, the Executive resigned. The exercise proves that consensus is not created by institutions, and that, where a majority of the population are strongly opposed to particular constitutional arrangements, these cannot be maintained. The Northern Ireland Protestants, like the Greeks, wanted majoritarianism, while the Catholics, like the Turkish Cypriots, wanted proportionality and effective minority vetoes.

The Lebanese National Pact of 1943, operating until 1975, required communities to be equitably represented in government. Cabinet posts were allocated on a confessional basis, convention requiring the President to be a Maronite Christian, the Prime Minister a Sunni Moslem, and the Chairman of Parliament a Shiite.

The proportion of six Christians to five Moslems was followed in the cabinet as in the Chamber of Deputies. The cabinet elites also engaged in inter-confessional deals, avoided conflict or affronting their own communities, and relied on the operation of mutual vetoes. Consequently there was little coherent policy, future planning or development of national attachments. When the geographic situation of the Lebanon is considered in the context of pan-Arabism, the presence of Palestinian refugee groups, and contiguity to Israel and Syria, it is astounding that the Lebanon for so long remained united through its Machiavellian political bargaining.

Only in Switzerland has power sharing developed organically over a century. The constitution provides for a seven man Federal Council holding office for a fixed term of four years. By convention proportional representation is used by the Federal Assembly to elect Council members. Any member of either house of the Swiss parliament elected to be a Federal Councillor must resign as the executive is independent of parliament. Representativeness is secured by the rule that no canton may provide more than one member of the seven man Federal Council. The effect is that there are usually four or five German-speakers, one or two French-speakers and one Italian-speaker. Power sharing, with voluntary acceptance of the principle of proportionality and the stable fixed-time coalition, together with an attitude of compromise prevalent since 1874, has resulted in relatively good intercommunal relationships.

Informal power sharing by coalition groups Coalition politics may develop where proportional representation voting systems apply, because frequently the proportionality principle ensures that no single group (provided ethnic groups are not grossly unequal in size) obtains an absolute majority. The power sharing arrangements in the Lebanon and Switzerland are partly formal and partly informal. In Holland and Belgium relatively stable coalition governments have been the usual voluntary practice. Their politics have been described as 'the politics of accommodation'. The combination of a PR voting system and groups so large that if domination is attempted the minority can retaliate by inflicting an unacceptable degree of damage on the majority seems to have led to a relationship of cooperation and mutual deterrence. Mutual vetoes are accorded in the constitutional amendment arrangements and even in case of some legislation—as under the alarm bell procedure in Belgium.

Malaysia also exemplifies the mutual deterrence model of ethnic community relations, again applying where the communities are approximately equal in numbers and able to operate mutual vetoes. The Alliance Coalition, between the major Malay and Chinese political parties, followed in 1972 by the National Front Coalition, led to a relative submergence of communal divisions. Assisting this is the 1971 constitutional provision prohibiting discussion of 'sensitive' issues. Similarly the enactment in Belgium in 1970 of constitutional policies safeguarding language removed this issue from the day to day sphere of knock-about politics. This phenomenon has been described as depoliticisation.

Formal recognition of minority language interests in the cabinet Formal recognition that 'minority' language speakers should play a role in executive government is found in the Belgian constitution. Since 1970 equal numbers of French-speaking and Flemish-speaking Ministers are required.

Informal recognition of minority language interests in the cabinet Convention requires the appointment to the Swiss Federal Council of five

German-speakers and one or two French-speakers, and one Italian speaker. Similar principles apply in Canada (where there is no PR and government is not by coalition) to the party in office. By convention the Canadian cabinet has at least one Minister from each Province and four from Quebec, one of whom must be English speaking.

Functional communalism in the cabinet Sometimes where problems particularly affect one community, it is arranged that the problem will be within the ministerial sphere of a Minister from that community. In the United Kingdom it is usual that the Secretary of State for Wales be a Welshman and that the Secretary of State for Scotland be a Scotsman. The procedure of using an 'ethnic representative' to settle divisive issues has also been employed in India (language issues in Southern India were thus dealt with in 1965).

Formal advisory bodies Ethnic or regional communities may be involved in executive decision making by setting up policy advisory bodies acting also as channels of communication. This was why the Council for Wales and Monmouthshire was formed in 1948. It is the progenitor of any Welsh Assembly (envisaged for the future under the United Kingdom government devolution policy). Similar bodies have been established in India and Nigeria to deal with intra-regional minorities.

Assistance to organisations Another method of encouraging long run pluralism, is to give financial or other assistance to bodies promoting good relations between persons of different groups. If unofficial such bodies become pressure groups seeking to influence executive government policies. Official bodies may also be established. Thus assistance under the Race Relations Act 1976 may be given by the Commission for Racial Equality as successor to other bodies.

THE CIVIL SERVICE

Administrative practice, rather than abstract legal provision, is the key both to individual liberty and protection of the interests of group members. In a plural society the composition and behaviour of the Civil Service are crucial to the real and perceived positions of minorities.

Civil Service employment opportunities favouring members of particular racial groups, either by according them preferences in employment or by fixing quotas, were discussed earlier. Such quotas or preferences are designed to maintain the proportional power balance between groups, and to encourage minority groups at the receiving end of state services to perceive the distribution of the spoils of state as fair and as being likely to ensure that they will themselves be fairly handled by the administration. To avoid fears of domination by a Civil Service, staffed in the main by a majority ethnic group, constitutions have imposed quota requirements in respect of patterns of Civil Service membership (Lebanon, Belgium, Cyprus).

In contrast, the provisions in Malaysia, although allegedly protective against Chinese dominance, are used to ensure Malay domination by administrative fixing of a 4:1 Malay to Chinese ratio. On the other hand, Malaysia has adopted Civil Service techniques of management likely in the long run to assist communal accommodation. The Department of National Unity examines the impact of all government programmes. Training programmes are designed to alert administrators to communal problems and to change their role perceptions, so that they see themselves as managers of communal conflict, as system guiders and as enforcers of the rule of law, and not merely as passive observers of community conflicts. Administrators are taught to cultivate responsiveness, to be flexible in the use of discretion, to ensure that there are regular flows of information and information exchanges between the communities and themselves, and to structure opportunities for communication and bargaining between the communities.[8]

PERSONAL LAW PROTECTIONS

Many modern governments have accepted that in plural societies the personal law of the communities should be preserved. In Britain's African and Asian posessions the personal law systems governing family law, the law of succession and land laws were by and large retained. The imperial regime also set up special courts either under the traditional authorities or under a colonial office to administer the personal law. Independent states have often continued this policy of preserving laws affecting the family and religious laws affecting personal status. Some may even have separate personal law courts (India and Lebanon).

ADMINISTRATIVE PROTECTIONS FOR GROUPS

Administrative systems have been established for the protection of 'backward' people. They work in conjunction with keeping the backward community on land reserved for it against purchase by other races (India and Canada). Such administrations are generally motivated by idealism and concern for the welfare of the indigenous people.[9] Examples of such administrations are the United States' Bureau of Indian Affairs, the Canadian Department of Indian Affairs, the Native Affairs Department (now Internal Affairs) of Rhodesia, and in India the office of the Commissioner of Scheduled Castes and Scheduled Tribes.

CONCLUSIONS

After this catalogue of constitutional styles tentative generalisations are possible. Distinctive geopolitical, attitudinal and institutional factors appear to accompany the treatment of minorities in a particular state (see accompanying table). One geopolitical factor is the relative sizes of majority and minority groups. If more or less equal in size, groups are in a 'no win' situation and compromise is the only alternative to constant battle. There is no mutual deterrence and little inducement to compromise or enter into co-operative arrangements where they are unequal in size or power. Another factor is whether a country is adjacent to a neighbouring state which supports the minority, or which is perceived as a threat to the majority. Then majority and minority are unlikely to reach an accommodation. The changing state of economic development is also crucial. If the country is industrialised and scarcity of resources does not trigger group competition relative harmony is more likely. If, in contrast, resources are scarce or the country is undergoing rapid economic modernisation with population migration conflict is more likely.

Another major factor affecting attitudes is the kind of cultural difference between majority and minority groups. Religious, ethno-linguistic, tribal, caste and nationality differences are all divisive. If they coincide, they are more likely to result in an ideology, and if this is developed, compromise is less likely (principle always being the enemy of peace). Nationalism is an exclusivist ideology: if the majority are chauvinistic they seek unchallenged hegemony, adopt majoritarian attitudes and are unwilling to make concessions; if the minority are nationalistic they prefer secession and their own rule.

Majority attitudes can thus be broadly categorised as majoritarian, compromising or even concessive. Conversely minority attitudes can be broadly classified as compromising or militant, even possibly secessionist.

Obviously geopolitical factors come first, and then attitudes, and lastly institutional arrangements. But the latter can markedly affect attitudes and eventual outcomes, while even geopolitical factors can be affected by a combination of attitudes and the provision of new institutions (the agreement between Italy and Austria, while possible agreement between the United Kingdom and Ireland and between Cyprus, Turkey and Greece could in the long term change the majority/minority relationships in two troubled areas).[10]

Institutional arrangements can be identified which seem to regulate and damp down conflict in multicultural societies.[11] Obviously there had first to be the motivation to introduce the arrangements but once introduced such arrangements have progressively been accompanied by accommodating attitudes as between majority and minority groups although previously such attitudes were absent.

Some of these arrangements are assimilationist and some pluralist. They include: adoption of the equality and non-discrimination principles by using some of the legal devices which secure equality; federal arrangements; proportional representation voting systems; executives outside the legislature (hence more independent and making it easier for elites to co-operate); coalition arrangements formal and informal; mutual vetoes *de facto* or *de jure*; depoliticisation by insulating certain issues in a relatively untouchable rigid constitution; equal access to central and local government service or the application of fair proportional quotas; organisation of the police and armed forces so that they are not perceived as being dominated by the majority group;

TABLE 7.1 Significant factors and attitudes in 12 states with major communal divisions

	Belgium	*Holland*	*Switzerland*	*Austria-Carinthia and Styria*	*Yugoslavia*	*Italy-South Tyrol*	*Canada-Quebec focussed*	*Cyprus*	*Lebanon*	*Northern Ireland*	*Sri-Lanka*	*Malaysia*
Geopolitical factors												
Groups about equal in size	+	+	+	–	–	–	–	–	Population ratio now i.f.o. Muslims	–	–	+
No neighbour problems	+	+	+	+	+	Until 1969	Perceived as threat	–	–	–	?	–
Kinds of communal division	Ethno-linguistic	Religious	Ethno-linguistic	Ethno-linguistic nationalism	Ethno-linguistic	Ethno-linguistic pan-nationalism	Ethno-linguistic nationalism	Ethno-linguistic pan-nationalism	Religious pan-nationalism	Nationalism Religious Ethnic	Ethno-linguistic Religious nationalism	Ethno-linguistic Religious
Attitudes												
No majoritarian approaches	+	+	+	+	+	+	–	–	+	–	–	+
Compromising approaches	+	+	+	+	+	+	–	–	+	–	–	+
Concessive approaches by majority	+	+	+	+	+	+	–	–	+	–	–	+
No secessionist attitudes	+	+	+	–	Not currently expressed	Not since 1969	From Canadian Confederation	–	+	–	–	+
Legal arrangements												
Equality and non-discrimination principles	+	+	+	+	+	+	+	+	+	Since 1970 only	Affirmative action i.f.o. majority	Affirmative action i.f.o. majority
Federation/regional type arrangements	Agreed 1970	–	+	+	+	+	+	–	–	–	–	+
Executive outside legislature	–	+	+	–	–	–	–	–	–	–	–	–
Proportional voting systems	+	+	+	+	One-party	Since 1972	–	+	+	Since 1972	–	–
Coalition-formal and informal	+	+	+	+ until 1965	One-party	Since 1972	–	Imposed	Not since 1974	Imposed	–	+
Mutual vetoes—*de jure* and *de facto*	+	+	+	+	+	+	Constitution imposed	Constitution imposed	Altered by PLO and Syrian presence	Legally imposed	–	+
Depoliticisation	+	+	+	+	+	+	Constitution seeks to do so	Constitution abandoned	–	Legal powers removed by UK Parliament	–	+
Equal access to central and local government services or fair proportional quotas	+	+	+	+	+	Proportionate quotas	+	Quotas imposed	Proportionate quotas	Since 1970 for local Government	–	Affirmative action i.f.o. majority
Army and police not dominated by majority group	+	+	+	–	+	–	–	Separate communal forces *de facto*	–	–	–	–
Equal linguistic treatment	+	+	+	+	+	+	+	+	+	N/A	–	–
State recognition and funding of communal schools	+	+	+	+	+	+	+	+	+	+	–	–

Key plus sign = yes; minus sign = no.

equal official treatment of languages; and state recognition and funding of communal schools. Table 7.1 applies these criteria to a number of multicultural societies. It reveals that the more intense the conflict the fewer of these devices are present, and that the more of the devices are present the more accommodating are the attitudes of the communities. The table shows visually by plusses that better inter-group relations seem to accompany particular factors and devices.

No abstract nostrums compounded of constitutional devices for societies with cultural minorities can however be prescribed. Law is always the product of politics.

NOTES

* This chapter is an expanded version of the report originally written by Professor Palley for the Minority Rights Group, entitled *Constitutional Law and Minorities*, of which copies are obtainable (price 5p), together with other reports on minorities' issues, from MRG, 36 Craven Street, London WC2N 5NG.

1. My frame of reference for defining minority groups is their relative power position in a society. Normally the most numerous groups are the most powerful, but if a group, although numerically a majority, is relatively powerless and dominated by a smaller group with greater force and technology at its command then I consider the former to be functionally a minority. In this sense the African tribal groups in South Africa are minorities *vis-à-vis* European South Africans. Where the geographical boundaries of power are drawn will also affect which group is or is not a minority. Thus French Canadians are a minority in Canada but a majority in Quebec, and Catholic Irishmen are a minority in Northern Ireland but a majority in the island of Ireland as a whole.
2. My use of 'pluralism' differs from that of Mr Gladdish in that it covers not only the pluralist solutions he describes, but also his differential solutions.
3. Where there is discretion i.e. choice as to whether to adopt alternative courses of action, whether it be in respect of search, interrogation, arrest, prosecution, judicial decision making or sentencing, it is possible for officials not merely to make wrong decisions, but also to abuse their position.
4. A. V. Dicey, *The Law of the Constitution* (London, Macmillan, 1965), p. 143.
5. W. S. Livingstone, *Federalism and Constitutional Change* (Oxford, 1956), pp. 1–2.
6. Although Belgium is not a federation yet, and was clearly a unitary state before 1970, willingness to strike a constitutional bargain and to move to a pre-federal pattern has so far prevented its fragmentation into Walloon and Flemish states.
7. For fuller details see A. E. Alcock, *Protection of Minorities—Three Case Studies:*

South Tyrol, Cyprus, Quebec (Belfast: The Northern Ireland Constitutional Convention, September 1975).

8. See M. J. Esman, *Administration and Development in Malaysia: Institution Building and Reform in a Plural Society* (Syracuse, 1972).
9. Depending upon the viewpoint of the observer protective measures will appear misguided, destructive or exploitative. Policies have included intervention to encourage assimilation; actions designed to acculturate and even sometimes to destroy the indigenous peoples; displacement so as to open up their land for exploitation; segregation designed to preserve peoples in their pristine state uncontaminated by modernising influences; and measures to assist and to encourage self-determination by the indigenous communities. Policies of protection and integration may of course be run in harness.
10. This paper dealt only with municipal law approaches and not with international law, which is an immense subject in itself and is touched on in Dr Alcock's paper.
11. A study of Belgium since 1830, Holland between 1890 and 1917, Switzerland in the nineteenth century, Austria between 1945 and 1965, and contemporary Malaysia and the Lebanon by Professor Nordlinger led him to conclude that in societies such as those, where sheer coercion is not possible, if intense conflicts are to be successfully regulated, one or more of six conflict-regulating practices is always employed. The six practices are the stable coalition, the proportionality principle, depoliticisation, the mutual veto, compromise, and concessions by the stronger to the weaker party. Such policies could be successfully employed only by political elites who could directly involve themselves in the conflict-regulating practices. He rejected as ineffective and counter-productive deliberate attempts to create a national identity. He dismissed any hypothesis that cross-cutting cleavages (such as membership of a church, a trade union, a profession) would effectively lessen inter-group conflict. He also thought socio-economic modernisation intensified conflicts. Professor Nordlinger's theory was designed to cover class as well as ethnic cleavages.
    E. A. Nordlinger, *Conflict Regulation in Divided Societies*, Occasional Papers in International Affairs, no. 29 (Boston: Harvard University Centre for International Affairs, 1972).

8 The Political Dynamics of Cultural Minorities

K. R. Gladdish

The position of minorities in multicultural states can be approached from a variety of different perspectives. Two important perspectives which bear upon questions of political interaction and adjustment are adopted elsewhere in this volume. They are worth summarising before a third perspective, which will be the setting of this chapter, can be introduced.

In the preceding chapter, Professor Palley outlines a constitutional concern with minority rights. Her approach rests upon the conviction that minorities, defined essentially as subordinate groups within a polity, are vulnerable to discrimination, exploitation and suppression by those who control the state and its resources. It therefore follows that minorities require protection by legal and constitutional provision if their members are to enjoy the same civil liberties and range of benefits as other citizens of the polity.

This perspective is inherently universalist in its concerns and prescriptions. Its assessment of the needs of any given situation arises from a specification of what should be common to all members of the polity. The task is then to calculate how best this can be ensured *despite* group distinctiveness. It does not, other than by further elaboration, enter directly into the dynamics of inter-group relations in terms of the ebb and flow of minority perceptions, initiatives and strategies. From the standpoint of this perspective the political arena thus becomes a forum for constitutional observance and the implementation of the formalised rules designed to protect minority members.

In an earlier chapter Dr Alcock adopts a different perspective, though the outcome may approximate to that of the constitutional approach. His starting point is the belief that it is the distinctive cultural properties and values of minorities which are the key priority and must be protected. The multicultural state on this view is regarded as a crucible within which distinctive minority cultures risk dissolution unless safeguarded against the dominant values of the majority. The prescriptions offered will, as before, tend to be legal and constitutional, though the less formal processes of political bargaining may not be excluded.

Both the *constitutional* and *cultural protectionist* perspectives are concerned with the preservation of certain values, in the first case individual rights and, in the second, cultural integrity. Both approaches reflect and express understandable anxiety and doubt whether these values can be safeguarded within a multicultural state by the exercise of political options on the part of minority groups and by the bargaining processes of political accommodation. Even where it might be acknowledged that political agencies can operate so as to adjust claims and concede issues, advocates of minority protection would contend that wherever the parties are unequal in size and strength, bargaining and adjustment must be guided by a commitment to the upholding of rights and the preservation of distinctive cultures.

There is much to be said for these concerns, which few would dismiss as irrelevant or invalid. But the framework of political arrangements within multicultural states has determinants which go beyond either individual rights or cultural protection. If we were to examine any sample of actual cases where minority questions arise, whether in South East Asia, North America or the peripheral regions of western Europe, we should find that these concerns are expressed in differing ways depending upon the particular relationship which is sought with the rest of the polity. And it is the need for some assessment of the operational aspects of minority/majority relationships which dictates the need for a third perspective—that of *political dynamics*.

It is scarcely possible to present an analysis of the political dimension of minority/majority relationships without attempting some general definition of what is meant by a multicultural state. Examples of what seem to be such states abound; indeed the mono-cultural state could be regarded as a comparatively rare phenomenon, though that also depends upon a clear definition. Unfortunately it is not at all easy to make a simple differentiation between mono- and multicultural polities. The difficulty arises primarily because any operational definition will need to relate to behaviour; but a behavioural criterion will not necessarily satisfy the range of possible grounds on which cultural distinctiveness and minority status might be adduced.

This is more than a definitional problem. It extends to the key conceptual question of how we can perceive and identify minorities. One could offer as an analytical datum the proposition that a minority only engages a political dimension when it makes claims for itself or its members which are distinctive from other claims within the polity. Distinctive, that is, in that they are made by and in the interests of a particular group. They may in fact be distinctive in their nature, e.g. the right to use a particular language, or to have special institutions. They may alternatively be concerned with properties which other groups already possess, e.g. equal rights, access to the national educational system, etc.

But there are many examples of situations where groups are regarded and regard themselves as minorities, yet for a variety of possible reasons do not make claims of an overtly political kind.[1] And there are other cases where groups may be treated as minorities—even though they may wish not to be so treated—without any recognition that they are entitled to make distinctive political claims. There is also the need to distinguish between informal social responses towards a minority, and the more formalised responses of public policy.

These elementary points already suggest a more bewildering canvas than the specification multicultural state may at first conjure up. There are further complications which must be cited. One is the assumption, which is common to both the constitutional and the cultural protectionist perspectives, that minorities are *ipso facto* in a defensive position *vis-à-vis* the rest of the polity. But that is strictly an operational question, because there are a large number of variables which determine whether minorities assume a defensive or an offensive position in relation to the polity.

Yet another problem is that it may not be possible to regard and treat the multicultural state as a single category. Because if we were to try to construct a typical model of such a state it would quickly become apparent that there is an extended spectrum of possible forms and that the spectrum might well be discontinuous. In Europe for example a typical feature of political formation has been the gradual evolution of sizeable states around a metropolitan core, originally heterogeneous in ethnic and cultural terms but eventually becoming largely homogenous with a dominant culture shared by the great majority of citizens. Many of these states, however,—France,[2] Britain, Spain,[3] etc. —contain within their boundaries regions, often peripheral, which are either culturally distinctive or retain some distinctive historic identity.[4] There are often additionally within states of this kind, immigrant and migrant groups of varying status and significance, which are not territorially sited or concentrated.

Elsewhere in the world, most notably in Africa, there are states at a much earlier stage of nation building which may consist of a whole galaxy of distinctive ethnic groups with as yet no dominant, metropolitan majority culture. Both kinds of state are clearly not mono-cultural. But to put both into a single operational category, as the blanket term multicultural might imply, is unlikely to yield a clear framework for analysis.

Having introduced a major variable—the differing complexions and composition of multicultural states—we may as well unpack some of the others. One is the salient question of the type or nature of the particular regime. The relationship between the type of regime and the nature of the polity may or may not be convergent depending upon the history of the political community. This is a complicated question of political analysis which can be illustrated by considering how far the 'Third Reich' was a designation of a regime or of a polity. But clearly there are two polarically opposite situations in which a minority may find itself *vis-à-vis* a regime. One is where minorities have freedom to organise and mobilise politically if they wish, and to enter the electoral arena as distinct or auxiliary party formations; the other is where this facility is not available and pressure can be exercised only either very discreetly or subversively. In the latter case, pluralist options will not be available and the pursuit of differential solutions is unlikely to be a feasible strategy unless by insurrection or other violent means. Authoritarian, centralising states have on occasions met this problem by permitting mass emigration,[5] but coercive regimes are generally hostile to the conferment of autonomous privileges upon distinctive cultural groups.

Even in the former case where open mobilisation and competitive bargaining is not prohibited, the extent to which differential or even pluralist solutions are in practice available may well be governed by assumptions about the nature of the polity. This is an area of great complexity and again points up differences between informal social behaviour and identifiable public policy. But it is inescapable that the scope for minority groups to pursue the whole range of strategies is affected by assumptions on the part of the dominant group about the form and character of the political community. The recent debate in Britain about the future status of Scotland, and to a lesser extent Wales, engages very directly with beliefs about the central importance of the preservation of the unitary state. And a similar belief provides at least one source of public policy in relation to recent immigrants to Britain where, despite unease at the social level, cultural pluralism seems not a viable option given the conviction that England, at least, is historically, operationally and 'necessarily' a mono-cultural entity.

In terms of these very broad variables, a working definition of the multicultural state becomes a formidably elusive task. If one adds to the factors already mentioned variations in levels of economic development, complexities of social stratification, and the protean question of the multiple bases and forms of cultural distinctiveness, it is probable that no single definition will serve any rigorous analytical purpose.

It might however be possible to frame the conditions of what could be considered an 'ideal type' of multicultural state or polity in terms which would both serve the reality of political dynamics and satisfy the concerns of constitutional and cultural protectionists. It might thus constitute a model of reference for political communities where problems of multiculturalism occur and are recognised. The necessary conditions of such a model would be that the response to those problems should be based upon the acceptance of three fundamental propositions: the universalisation of individual rights, the validity of cultural values and properties which may differ from that of the dominant majority, and thirdly the commitment to the resolution of political and social claims by competitive bargaining and adjustment.

It is difficult to frame the latter two imperatives in terms which avoid any need for qualification or elaboration. There may be certain cultural values and beliefs which are regarded as simply unacceptable by a dominant majority; and a commitment to the resolution of claims within the political arena may not succeed in settling all disputes to the satisfaction of all claimants. But at least some specification of the 'acceptable' multicultural state becomes possible and could be phrased in the following terms: a polity containing groups whose members consider themselves to have a distinctive identity, and who are able to make claims on behalf of themselves individually, and of the group as a whole, which will be considered within the political arena and dealt with fairly as part of the normative operations of the state.

On a utilitarian assessment of the political motivation of minority groups there would seem to be two counterpoised stimuli: the sense of a threat to the position of the group and its members; and the perception of the advantages and disadvantages which might attend any positive innovative strategy. In the language of everyday reasoning, people will tend to act if a situation seems to be progressively deteriorating; they will also tend to act if important gains can be achieved. Within the broad middle ground between those two sensations, the behaviour of both groups and individuals will tend to be acquiescent.

There is a logistic dimension to both group and individual behaviour. There must be a belief that enough strength can be assembled to pursue either resistance or an aggressive strategy and these alternative positions may themselves be on an ascending scale. A battle to defend a position or rectify a grievance may extend into an offensive which challenges the whole relationship between a minority group and the polity.

A detailed elaboration of this process accompanied by a comprehensive examination of actual cases is beyond the scope of an outline review. But it may be illustrated by citing three cases within 'developed' states in the northern hemisphere, two of which are of contemporary relevance, the third of which is more historical. The cases in mind are Quebec separatism, Scottish nationalism and the political mobilisation of Catholics in the Netherlands, in the late nineteenth and early twentieth centuries.

The terms used to express these examples—separatism, nationalism, and mobilisation—are not typological; they are merely the most familiar. To list all the factors which figure in the three cases would yield a massive agenda of items. But if we refer only to factors already mentioned when considering the variables which affect the definition of the multicultural state, then the age of the polity, the nature of the regime, the pattern of centralising institutions and assumptions about the operation of the state would all need to be reviewed.

Predictable problems of comparability arise here. Britain, the Netherlands and Canada each subtend a different profile in terms of the history, anatomy and physiology of the overall polity and the relationship between it and minority groups. What is however common to the three cases is that at a certain point in time, the *status quo* which was peculiar to each was challenged on behalf of the so-called minority group by political activists who selected fresh goals and strategies. In the case of Scotland,[6] there was little evidence that a distinctive culture was under threat, but there were indications that advantages could be gained from a new relationship, or perhaps even the end of a direct political relationship, with the rest of the polity. In the case of Quebec,[7] the twin facets of a distinctive culture being progressively undermined and the advantages of a new status were combined in a strategy of separatism. In the case of the Dutch Catholic population in the latter half of the nineteenth century, there is evidence of a decreasing threat to religious distinctiveness, but clear indications that by mobilising politically and creating a denominational party which could operate at national level, considerable advantages would be gained by the group and its members.[8] Since at the critical point the Catholic population of the Netherlands was concentrated geographically in the two southern provinces of Limburg and Brabant, it is conceivable that there was an alternative possible strategy in terms of regional devolution. Alternative strategies are equally discernible in the cases of Scotland and Quebec, and may yet be engaged as the political process unfolds.

The points to be made are that although minority behaviour is clearly subject to logistic and environmental factors which limit options, strategies nevertheless change and are changeable, do not correlate in any predictable way with the intensity of particular cultural features, do nevertheless have an implicit basis in a calculus of threat and/or advantage, and above all depend upon political activists to select, articulate, advocate and finally operationalise them.

The moral of these uncertainties is that relationships between groups within the multicultural state are rather more volatile than the constitutional or cultural protectionist perspectives tend to allow for. How far any multicultural polity can be regarded as a stable entity thus depends upon a harmonisation of dynamic factors which may not be susceptible to either clear-cut or enduring formulations.

It is nevertheless necessary to consider what alternative patterns for the projection and reconciliation of group demands are available, and what each entails. From the vantage point of national politics the multicultural state confronts a finite number of possible strategies *vis-à-vis* minority groups. They can be assembled under three broad headings: *integrative strategies, pluralist recipes* and *differential formulae.*

Integrative strategies extend from positive policies of assimilation, with its many variables, to less clear-cut techniques of depoliticisation. Subjugation is also an alternative possibility under this heading and must be reckoned with. The essence of such strategies is to produce over time a polity which can be operated as though it were a mono-cultural entity. The object must therefore be to incorporate the members of all groups into the major political and social institutions and thereby remove group distinctiveness as a focus of political and allied claims. Residual patterns of distinctive group behaviour in terms of language, religion, ceremonies, etc. may however survive even thoroughgoing strategies of assimilation where the aim is other than to obliterate all features of cultural heterogeneity.

The second broad heading—*pluralist recipes*—covers a range of policies which recognise the presence within the polity of distinctive groups but seek to incorporate them within the national arena on a coalitional basis. Examples of what are generally regarded as successful pluralist strategies are afforded by the Proporz formula in the Austrian Republic post-1949,[9] and the 'politics of accommodation' which has characterised the working of the party system in the Netherlands since 1917.[10] A less successful, indeed so far unsuccessful, instance of the pluralist approach is the attempt to introduce a system of power sharing in Northern Ireland since 1973. This last example could serve as a negative illustration of what is required for pluralist recipes to work. There must clearly be a shared overall allegiance on the part of all participating groups, a commitment to the survival of the polity and a sufficient degree of acceptance of the institutions which form the arena for the exercise of coalitional politics.

The logistics of power sharing may not be capable of easy generalisation. In the Dutch case, where the arrangements have never been formalised, the Catholic party, originally conceived as the agency of a minority group, has been until very recently the leading political formation. Less advantaged minorities, in terms of demography and resources, may not so readily be admitted to a power sharing formula unless other strategies have either failed or proved too costly.

The third general heading—*differential solutions*—involves the formal recognition that distinctive groups can be accommodated within the polity only if accorded distinctive institutions. Here the range of available nostrums extends from federal systems down to special arrangements for minority groups at the most local levels of administration.

These differing approaches to incorporation can all be regarded as alternative modes of pursuing a universal aim—the creation and underpinning of a stable polity. The need to incorporate distinctive groups by some process or other is an imperative which all states confront. It is not simply or solely a matter of preserving the framework of an overall political community. The effective harnessing of the economic and human resources of the polity requires a formula for successful incorporation. Political stability depends upon a reliable system for preventing unrest and coping with the special demands which may be created directly or indirectly by the presence of distinctive groups.

The necessity of a uniform legal order, the disadvantages of costly security operations on an indefinite basis, the stabilisation of inter-group competition, the neutralising of dissident elites—all of these needs provide powerful motivations for the achievement of a dependable recipe for incorporation.

But from the standpoint of the minority groups which confront these variant policies, the outcome in each case is clearly very different. Integrative or assimilationist strategies have the Manichaean property of representing either the conferment of a status enthusiastically sought by sections of a population which had formerly felt dispossessed, persecuted and discriminated against, or the annihilation of a cultural heritage and a way of life considered central to communal well-being, self-respect and fulfilment.[11]

The pursuit of assimilation by a minority is a likely strategy only where the gains in status and access to what the majority presides over seem more rewarding than the retention of a distinctiveness conferring low status, lack of access and perhaps unpleasant forms of discrimination. Here ethnic factors may differentiate themselves from other cultural properties. Ethnic differentiation is unlikely to be rewarding to a minority where a majority controls the polity. But distinctions which are seen as primarily ethnic rather than cultural are the most difficult to transcend by an assimilationist strategy.

Where a valued cultural heritage is at stake, the quest for assimilation by a minority may be partial in that it seeks the access, and if available, the status, but does not wish to forfeit all distinctiveness. In such cases if the logistics are favourable, the pursuit of pluralist formulae may be more attractive. Because among the political implications of assimilationist tactics is the possibility that minority elites may lose their role unless fully incorporated in the new arena, whilst majority elites may forfeit a part of their 'ideological' base.

The feasibility of pluralist strategies depends upon a number of favourable ingredients. Issues on which groups differ must be bargainable; all elites must be rewarded; elite-mass relations within each group must be safeguarded; and the commitment to pluralist accommodation must be long-term, because the mechanisms may need to be elaborate and may need time to evolve. Where the arrangements are formalised this may impede future adjustments to subsequent changes in logistic or power relationships.

In the case of differential solutions the commitments are even more profound. Resources must be divided up; the direct jurisdiction of majority rule will need to be curtailed; group distinctiveness or regional autonomy or whatever may be the basis of the differentiated unit must be given constitutional recognition; elaborate co-ordination of services and agencies may be necessary; and finally territorial sovereignty may be fragmented.

This highly generalised review of the consequences of different strategies draws attention to the central importance of political elites.[12] Integrative solutions rely for their ultimate success upon an effective absorption of existing and putative elites into the central political structure. Pluralist and certain of the differential solutions call for the continuous co-operation of distinctive elites at national level. The achievement of stable patterns of elite co-operation in these latter cases will depend upon the fulfilment of certain basic conditions.

First, each distinctive group will need to be served by an elite which can represent its particular character, effectively express its needs at the political level, secure benefits for the group, and behave co-operatively within the national arena.

Secondly, each distinctive elite will itself need to be rewarded both within the group and at the national level. The politics of accommodation has been described as a system in which everyone continuously receives prizes. Which is to say that it is an arrangement dependent upon the removal of tension by continuous gratification, primarily of elites.

Thirdly, the particular strength and status of each distinctive group must be continually monitored. This is because a peaceful, stable *modus vivendi* requires adjustments to be made if there are significant changes in the relative position of each group.

Each of these conditions can be amplified. Most multicultural societies must be viewed as kaleidoscopic in that the elements which make up the pattern are in a state of continual change *vis-à-vis* each other. Patterns of accommodation may be developed which reasonably accurately express the relative size, status, economic importance and special needs of each component group. The factors may then change, either objectively or subjectively. Differential birth rates or uneven economic development would be obvious examples of objective change. But the demands of groups may also change, and the leadership of groups may be subjected to considerable strain if unable to translate changes in group demands into the securing of increased benefits.

Changes in group demands may be, and very frequently are, the result of stimulation on the part of new, putative leaders who may seek to change existing accommodation patterns. In these circumstances the leadership at the level of national bargaining may cease to be synonymous with the leadership at the expressive level of mass demands or dissatisfaction.[13] The two kinds of leadership may be of different generations, and the newer may express a completely different conception of the role of the group within the polity.

There are in fact a number of possible patterns which can be traced where changes in the relationship between groups, however triggered off, may affect the position of established elites. But there are perhaps two major alternative models. The first can be set out in two stages in Figure 8.1.

The separation of established elites from their mass base is a phenomenon which is not of course confined to the multicultural polity. All competitive politics in societies of any scale exhibit features of accommodation between rival elites at national level.

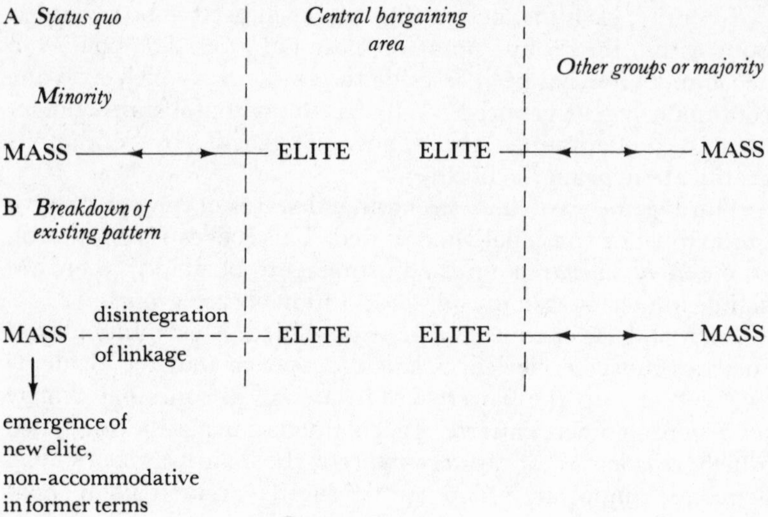

FIGURE 8.1

The processes and rewards of accommodation tend always to separate elites from those whom they represent.

One of the distinctive properties of a multicultural society is that the mass membership of groups may retain their separate identity more readily than accommodative leaderships—which may gradually merge into a national 'establishment', secure in its own terms, rewarded more by prizes within the central bargaining arena than by its followers. Provided groups remain cohesive, the position of accommodative elites can always therefore be challenged by new, aspirant leaders with fresh recipes for group strategy.

The second model of the effects upon elite behaviour of changing relationships between groups is one in which the pattern of accommodation is either severed or disrupted by a retreat of elites from the central arena. The retreat could be either unilateral or multilateral, i.e. it could affect either one elite or all elites, and could be brought about either by strains at the central bargaining level or by strains at the mass base.

The prospect of disaccommodation confronts any polity committed to an over-arching elite or power sharing formula. This possibility of strains in elite-mass relations underlines the risks inherent in such formulae and draws attention to one of the underlying problems inherent in the operation of a multicultural state.

Multicultural societies may be regarded as facts of political geography which must be respected and coped with either because they are unalterable or because there are positive values in multiculturalism which ought to be protected. But there is of course a quite different position which can be adopted—the mono-cultural or nationalist position. This, a familiar enough standpoint, would hold that each distinctive group has a right to and a need for its own polity. This alternative stance will be briefly reviewed as the final theme of this chapter on the grounds that many multicultural states contain nationalistic minorities, and that the strategy of separatism must be included in the catalogue of options which may be taken up by certain minorities.[14]

The starting point of the nationalist or mono-cultural position is the conviction that group distinctiveness cannot be satisfied within a multicultural polity. Such a conviction may be absolute in that it would not matter what other groups were included in the polity nor what their attitudes and policies were. Mono-cultural solutions may also be sought because of the unsatisfactory nature of relations with other groups within the polity.

Two sets of factors govern the adoption of mono-cultural formulae. The first might be called qualifying, in the sense that certain conditions have to be met before a separatist strategy becomes even a theoretical possibility. Under this heading one can group all the factors which underpin a compelling, collective sense of group distinctiveness—an historic identity, cultural properties, an economic framework which offers the prospect of viability (though this is a hard criterion to specify) and probably the possession of institutions which can form the basis of a new and separate state. There are also obvious geographical needs which can be catalogued under the same heading: a separable and acquirable territory, access to international communications, etc.

The satisfaction of these criteria does not automatically generate the necessary momentum for the pursuit of separate statehood. There is a further set of operational factors which are of the same kind as those already reviewed when examining the strategies available within the framework of multi-cultural solutions. If the hinge on which most mono-cultural solutions turn is a conviction that relations with other groups in a polity cannot be satisfactorily or beneficially maintained, then the articulation of this conviction becomes the task of the political leadership of the disaffected group. There is no other way that the conviction can be assembled, expressed or translated into action.

This factor of elite response seems to transcend not only ethno-cultural distinctiveness but indeed all other variables as a determinant of separatist dispositions. In accounts of separatism in societies as diverse as the Sudan, Bangladesh and Biafra, the intensity of secessionist pressures has been represented as highly dependent upon the extent to which the respective elites believed that the accommodation of their ambitions within a centralising polity was possible.

Quotations from two such accounts express this point vividly.[15] In his summary of the sequence in Bangladesh, Mizanur Rahman reports:

> The glorification of Bengali culture and language in the fifties and sixties was entirely the work of the middle classes. With only 17 per cent of the region's population literate, the fine disputes about cultural assertion and autonomy could not be of much interest and significance to the peasant masses. But the elite used these to great advantage in underlining the distinction and differences between East Bengal and West Pakistan.
>
> Nevertheless, on account of the participation—however limited—that the Bengali political elite obtained in this period, it modified its strident demand for Bengali regionalism during this time and contributed to making this 'a most creative' period of 'integrative institution-building'. The measure of the success of the integrative political process in this period is the moderation in the role of the chief exponents of Bengali regional autonomy in the early fifties.

The importance of accommodating the elites in the southern Sudan, and the variations of strategy on the part of both secessionists and the central government are brought out in R. K. Badel's account of *The Rise and Fall of Separatism in Southern Sudan.*

> Southern separatism vacillated between demands for local self-rule and the extreme of outright secession . . . the perceptions and expectations of (the most articulate elements) had largely been responsible for the shaping of Southern demands . . . to contain secessionist sentiments these Southern aspirants to power have to be accommodated. This is precisely the course

of action President Numeiry chose to follow in an attempt to face up to the Southern challenge.

To conclude, the key political factors in the assembly and maintenance of the multicultural state can be presented as a sequence of points. The first is the question of what position each minority chooses to advance or protect *vis-à-vis* the polity, and its obverse—what kind of accommodation the dominant or majority group is willing and able to concede. Secondly there are the operational variables which attend the selection of particular strategies by the various component groups; and allowance has to be made here for the fact that strategies may be pursued on different levels and may change in response to variations in both subjective and objective assessments. Thirdly there are the structural factors which affect the feasibility and likely outcome of any chosen pattern of incorporation. Finally there is the all-pervading need for elites to be accommodated within that pattern.

The frame of what has been called in this chapter 'political dynamics' can contribute to the organisation of these factors in a way which ought at least to illuminate the possibilities, and highlight the logistic, structural and operational obstacles and limitations. Each actual situation is however unique and what is acceptable to minority and majority groups will not be settled by the conceptualisations of political science. That can be determined only by the participants themselves.

NOTES

1. In most European societies Jewish populations have tended not to make overtly political claims on the polity. Immigrant groups generally will tend to adopt a low political profile; and wherever there is a history of conquest followed by repression even minorities with a territorial base may well prefer acquiescence to the framing of distinctive political demands.
2. Among recent studies, see J. Hayward, 'Institutionalised Inequality within an Indivisible Republic', *Journal of the Conflict Research Society*, vol. 1, part 1 (August 1977).
3. An excellent analysis of peripheral nationalism in Spain is contained in the chapter by J. Linz on 'Early State-building and late Peripheral Nationalisms against the State: the Case of Spain' in Eisenstadt and Rokkan (eds.), *Building States and Nations*, vol. II (Sage, 1973).
4. An impressive recent analysis of peripheral nationalism is provided by A. W. Orridge, *Peripheral Nationalisms* (Berlin: European Consortium for Political Research Workshops, March-April 1977).

5. Tsarist Russia in the late nineteenth century permitted Jews to emigrate rather than grant them either cultural protection or the assurance of full civil rights.
6. An impressive study amid the recent spate of writing on Scottish nationalism is K. Webb, *The Growth of Nationalism in Scotland* (Molendinar Press, 1977).
7. Recent studies of Quebec separatism include two papers by J. E. Trent, *Nationalist and Class Interests in Multi-Ethnic Countries: the Case of Nationalist Groups in French Canada*, University of Ottawa Working Paper no. 5 (1975); and *The Causes of Nationalist Movements; the Case of French Canada in the 1960s*, (Louvaine-la-neuve: European Consortium for Political Research Workshops, April 1976).
8. See J. M. G. Thurlings, 'The Case of Dutch Catholicism: A Contribution to the Theory of the Pluralistic Society', *Sociologia Neerlandica*, vol. III, No. II (1971). This article also contains some interesting general analysis of minority behaviour in a form which elaborates the threat/advantage hypothesis referred to in this chapter.
9. For a succinct account of this arrangement see F. C. Englemann, 'Austria: The Pooling of Opposition' in R. A. Dahl, *Political Oppositions in Western Democracies* (Yale, 1966).
10. A. Lijphart, *The Politics of Accommodation* (University of California, 2nd ed., 1975).
11. The oscillation of responses by minorities to integrative politics is well illustrated by the history of black consciousness in the USA, where, after generations of patient hope for assimilation, there was a violent swing in the 1960s towards assertions of ethnic distinctiveness and demands for its recognition. For a review of Black Power groups and tactics, see A. Pinkney, 'Contemporary Black Nationalism' in R. L. Goldstein, *Black Life and Culture in the United States* (New York, 1971).
12. K. Deutsch, *Nationalism and Social Communication* (New York, 1953), was an early writer to stress the importance of elite incorporation for national integration. Linz and Miguel refer to him in their critique of national unity in Spain, and contend that 'it might well be that the social, cultural and political integration of a society depends on the degree of homogeneity or differentiation of the recruitment of its elites'. J. Linz and A. de Miguel, 'Within-National Differences and Comparisons: The Eight Spains', in Marriott and Rokkan (eds.) *Comparing Nations* (Yale, 1966).
13. This process is observable in the build-up of nationalist or quasi-nationalist pressures in Scotland, Wales and most dramatically in Northern Ireland. Quebec also exemplifies the phenomenon.
14. The assessments here are derived from the author's paper on 'Separatism' delivered at the ECPR Workshop on 'The Politics of Multicultural Societies' at Louvaine-la-neuve (April, 1976).
15. Both accounts appear in 'The Politics of Separatism', *London University Institute of Commonwealth Studies Collected Seminar Papers*, no. 19 (1976), pp. 37–48 and 85–93.

9 Conclusions

The future of cultural minorities will depend on the future of the traditional or otherwise distinctive component in minority cultures. With the disappearance of the one will go that of the other.

(A) THE NATURE OF PRESENT-DAY MINORITY CULTURES

We have indicated how the culture of a minority, viewed as a sub-culture within a national culture, might be analysed, and how by reference to different dimensions—social organisation (groups and ways of life), technology and ideological systems (ways of thought)—related in turn to territorial location (regional and local communities) and to class, it is possible to identify the overall form of the culture and its national, sub-national and traditional or otherwise distinctive components.

In this way the characterisation of the minority culture-in-itself, and its relationship with other sub-cultures (majority or minority) in the nation is facilitated. For example, with regard to the former, one may determine the minority culture's *structural type*—simple, intermediate or complex, and the extent of its differentiation in different groups, communities and classes, its *level of development*—primitive, intermediate or advanced, and its *kin-culture* or historical cultural family—American Indian, Western European, Eastern European, Islamic, Bantu, Hindu, Far-Eastern, Polynesian or whatever.

With regard to its relationship with other sub-cultures in the nation one may establish the minority culture's *distinctiveness* both in general terms like structure, level of development and kin-culture already listed and also in specific terms by reference to detailed components in the organisational, technological and ideological dimensions. Here one discovers whether there are significant differences in, for example, the minority's domestic, linguistic, recreational, educational, economic, political, military, administrative, legal, scientific, religious, philosophical and artistic organisation, in their technology and in their ideology compared with those of others in the nation. Fixing the societal and territorial location of distinctive patterns is clearly important for its draws attention to the groups who maintain, transmit or adopt the distinctive culture—in other words those creators, controllers and conformists who are directly concerned with keeping it alive—and also to their whereabouts in different communities or classes where these exist. In some cases this may reveal that some of the distinctive culture is preserved by a minority of the minority, and that there are many non-conformists.

A second aspect is the relationship of the *non-distinctive* part of the minority culture with other sub-cultures in the nation-state. This concerns cultural components which the minority members 'share' with members of the other cultural collectivities (majority and/or minority). These shared patterns can together be taken as a preliminary indicator of the nature and degree of the minority culture's *consistency* with the total culture of the national population. The term 'cultural consistency' is here preferred to cultural integration because it embraces common patterns like the religious which may have been acquired prior to the minority's incorporation in the nation-state as well as those like the economic or recreational which may have resulted from a subsequent integration or 'coming together'. As with the distinctive so with the shared components, societal and territorial location can be profitably explored. The creators, controllers, conformists and non-conformists are identified. A development of this analysis will facilitate the positioning of the minority culture on a cultural dominance/subordination scale relative to other sub-cultures.

When this approach is applied to a selection of present-day minority cultures like those of the American Indians, French Canadians, Welsh, Scots, Bretons, Catalans, South Tyrolese, Turkish Cypriots, Zulus, Afrikaners, Ganda and Karamajong of Uganda, the Tamils of Sri Lanka and the Aborigines of Australia, what does one find?

Considering first the more general cultural characteristics one finds with regard to both structure and level of development that while half the minorities like the French Canadians, Welsh and Bretons are basically similar in type to other cultural collectivities in their nation-states the other half like the American Indians, Zulus, Ganda and Australian Aborigines are markedly different. In some cases, as in South Africa, one is reminded that a minority culture like the Zulu may be different from some other minority cultures like the Afrikaner while being similar to others in the same country like the Swazi. With regard to the other general characteristic, kin-culture, *all* of the minorities in the set examined have a distinctive historical cultural family compared with that of the majority or other minorities in the nation state. It was noted, however, that the degree of difference of the kin-cultures of collectivities in the different states varied. For example, the difference between the kin-cultures of French and English Canadians or between South Tyrolese and Italians is considerably less than that between Ganda and Karamajong, or between white and aboriginal Australians. In these general senses, therefore, there is varying scope for change as between minorities and other cultural collectivities in different countries, and as between such groups in the same country.

An important point about the present structure of minority cultures is that most—there are obviously exceptions like the Karamajong—are in themselves already differentiated as between groups, communities and classes. That is to say, division of labour, territorial mobility, education, urbanisation and concentration of wealth have reached such a point that within the minority (in most cases) there are detectable cultural variations as between members of different occupations, rural and urban communities and socio-economic classes. This structural complexity makes it all the more necessary to clarify if one is concerned about the future of minority cultures what part of that culture, in each case, and generally, one has in mind.

Returning to the relationship between minority cultures and other cultures in the society we examined first what in more specific dimensional terms—organisational, technological and ideological—was their present distinctiveness. There were difficulties here arising out of incomplete evidence—*all* the major patterns or systems of organisation, technology and ideology of *all* minorities are obviously not known—and a further difficulty of making a useful selection of indicators of distinctiveness—how, for example, with the evidence that *was* available was one to measure the distinctiveness of a minority's domestic or educational or economic or political organisation, its language, its technology, and its religious, political, historical or other ideology?

The following *indicators* of cultural distinctiveness were found to have initial manageability and value: in *domestic organisation*—distinctive marriage form (monogamy, polygamy, etc.), marriage prescriptions (exogamy, endogamy), marriage prestations (bridewealth, service, dowries), rule of descent (patrilineal, matrilineal, etc.), and rules governing the termination of marriage (divorce, separation, widow inheritance, levirate, etc). If distinctions finer than the presence or absence of these rules are required, and evidence can be gathered, the incidence of the practices, e.g. polygamy, payment of dowry, divorce, etc. can be calculated.

Indicators of *linguistic distinctiveness* were distinctive language type, distinctive home language, language of education, language of work and commerce, language of social life and sport, language of the mass media, language of government, language of the church and language of literature and the arts. Once again refined measures are possible, for example by reference to actual language use in different grades of educational institutions up to the most advanced.

Other indicators were, in *recreational organisation*: distinctive games and sports; in *educational organisation*: distinctive types of school, curricula and methods of instruction; in *economic organisation*: distinctive types of economic groups or organisations, system of property ownership, and types and methods of production, distribution and exchange, and consumption and investment.

Similar indicators of distinctiveness were used in the fields of *political, military, administrative, legal, scientific, religious, philosophical, mass media* and *artistic organisation, viz.* distinctive groups or organisations of the kinds mentioned, and distinctive types and methods or techniques or procedures of activity.

Indicators of *technological distinctiveness* were distinctive material equipment in the different industry groups of primary production, mining and quarrying; manufacturing; utilities and construction; transport and communication; commerce and finance; public administration and professional; entertainment, sport and recreation; and personal and domestic service.

Finally, useful indicators of *ideological distinctiveness* were distinctive systems of scientific, magical and religious, philosophical, artistic, historical, political and legal thought and expression. Here the focus was on the distinctive content, if any, of, for example, science, religion, art, law, political ideology and so on.

The application of this approach to the minority cultures selected reveals that the greater part of each culture, in most cases, was not distinctive. This non-distinctive part frequently included the major components, or the greater part of the major components of economic, political, governmental, military, administrative, legal, scientific, philosophical, mass media, artistic and recreational organisation, of material technology, and of economic, governmental, military, administrative, legal, scientific, philosophical, mass media and recreational ideology. These were similar in the minority culture and in the cultures of some or all of the other cultural collectivities in the state. The distinctive part of these minority cultures, on the other hand, frequently included the major components of linguistic organisation (i.e. language) and historical, artistic and political ideology and expression. In some cases also domestic, educational and religious distinctiveness with regard to both organisation and ideology might be marked.

These divisions are set out in simplified form in the accompanying diagram. Whether this division of distinctive/non-distinctive minority culture is representative of most minority cultures in the world others may explore. Our purpose here by directing attention to parts, dimensions and components is to facilitate, in the sections which follow, the analysis of the 'forces' at work in different areas of minority culture.

What should not be overlooked in the cultural situation described is the related and underlying social situation, that is the groups (in their territorial and class context) who control or enforce, conform to or adopt, do not conform to or adopt, seek to reform, or seek to create the distinctive or non-distinctive parts of the minority culture. Figure 9.1 provides pointers to some of these.

(B) FORCES ACTING ON PRESENT-DAY MINORITY CULTURES

In considering the forces acting on present-day minority cultures

Organisation	*Technology*	*Ideology*
	← *Frequently distinctive* →	
Language		Historical Artistic Political
	← *Intermediate* →	
(Sometimes distinctive/non-distinctive) Domestic Educational Religious		Domestic Educational Religious
	← *Frequently non-distinctive* →	
Economic Political Governmental Military Administrative Legal Scientific Philosophical Mass-media Artistic Recreational	Material Technology	Economic Governmental Military Administrative Legal Scientific Philosophical Mass-media Recreational

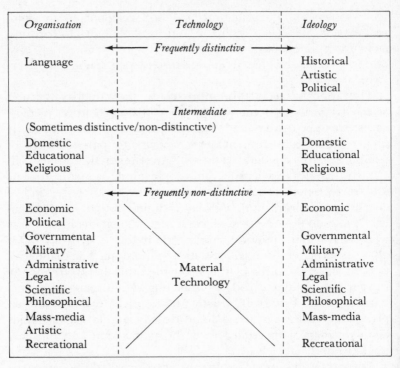

FIGURE 9.1 Distinctive and non-distinctive parts of minority culture

it is useful initially to use an even more simple model of a minority culture, that is one consisting of only two components, *viz.* a distinctive part and a non-distinctive part. We refer of course in each case to established or standardised and on-going or maintained ways-of-life, technology and ways-of-thought. These need no further specification at this stage.

Among the forces playing upon this active minority culture we are concerned primarily with the social. Social forces are here taken to be human group forces directed at influencing, or otherwise influencing, individual and social behaviour.

We have already drawn attention to some of the more influential groups who participate in the cultural process—the controllers (conservative or radical) who seek to enforce or transmit culture, the conformists and non-conformists who accept and adopt, or do not accept and adopt, this culture, and the creators who work at the production of new or modified cultural forms.

This emphasis on the force of the groups—a social force—rather than on the force of disembodied ideas and values, etc.—a cultural force—will be maintained. It is of course recognised that group influence may partly derive from the compelling 'force' of some idea or material instrument.

The different types of group referred to also remind us that what the members of a minority do in either their 'distinctive' culture or 'non-distinctive' culture is the resultant of many interacting group or social forces. It is important that these be thoroughly identified and their present and future relative strength be estimated. But how does one identify and measure the social forces involved?

At this stage it is helpful to reintroduce examples of the distinctive and non-distinctive parts of a minority culture. They might be language in the first case and, say, a pattern of factory management in the second, but the reader may prefer his own examples.

The approach we adopted to identification of social forces acting on any such chosen component of distinctive or non-distinctive minority culture was this. First, we tried to identify the forces conserving or preserving the component—these we called the *forces of conservation.* These might include (i) the users of the component, e.g. those who speak the language or employ the management system—we called these the conforming force; (ii) those who enforce the use of the component: this was the positive controlling force; (iii) those who in other ways assist the use of the component; this was the tradition-supporting force; and (iv) those who currently transmit the component to possible future users: this was the tradition-transmitting force.

After seeking to identify conservative forces of these kinds we secondly explored the existence of forces directed at changing, or otherwise changing, the component—these we called the *forces of change.* These might include (i) those aiming to modify the component: these we called the reforming force; (ii) the non-users of the component, e.g. those known by the users to be non-conformists: this was the non-conforming force; (iii) those who prohibit the use of the component: this was the negative controlling force; (iv) those who in other ways opposed the use of the component: this was the tradition-opposing force; and (v) those who currently transmit alternative components: this was the alternative-transmitting force.

This treatment immediately draws attention to the fact that the forces, conservative or changing, acting on a minority culture are both internal and external to the group of users of the cultural components concerned. This is represented in extremely simplified form in Figure 9.2.

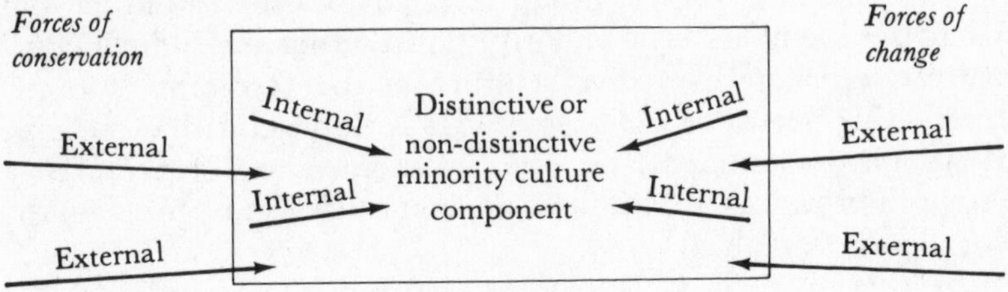

FIGURE 9.2 Social forces acting on a minority culture (Internal and external forces represented)

What of the measurement of the strength of these social or group forces? The approach we adopted was to distinguish a group's *power* in the sense of a potential based on command of various resources from its *force* in the sense of power actually applied, and from its *influence* in the sense of the effects of the force. This seemed essential for a powerful group does not necessarily apply much force to a particular situation, and whether it does or not, this force does not necessarily have much influence.

Possible indicators of group *power* or power potential based on command of resources were taken to be group size (membership), financial assets, political authority (government backing), power links (links with other powerful bodies), degree of power concentration (extent to which group dominates its field), knowledge and expertise (possession of a research and development unit) and moral authority (possession of accepted moral judgement).

Turning to group *force* in the sense of power actually exercised or applied we used as indicators: volume of output of messages (informative, persuasive and coercive) and of goods and services, the territorial range of this output (international, national, regional or local), length and continuity of output flow (relative to time periods and to life-stage periods and sub-periods like childhood, adolescent, adult and life-long periods), frequency of output flow (daily, weekly, monthly, etc.) and variations in the strength (volume) and territorial range of the flow over time. The last indicator was considered particularly important because it might reveal whether forces playing on minority cultures represented mounting, consistent or declining pressures.

When this approach to the identification and measurement of the forces acting on distinctive and non-distinctive components of a minority culture is applied to the selection of minority cultures previously listed what does one find?

It would appear that with regard to *power* there has in the present century in all the countries concerned been a considerable concentration of power in large economic, political (parties and trade unions), governmental (departments) and educational and mass communication organisations. In some of the countries, for example in Uganda, there has also been a concentration of power in religious organisations. These organisations have come to exert 'force' over large, usually nationwide, areas. A further development, in all the countries, has been an extension of governmental influence or control over the other forces. This framework of forces, and especially that of the governmental, economic, educational and mass communication systems, embraces the bulk of the population, majority and minorities alike. Not all of the major forces acting on present-day minority cultures are those of the large organisations described, however. Highly significant among the remainder is the confined but concentrated, primary, intimate, consistent and continuous force of the family or family network.

The forces identified act, in different combinations and sequences, upon different distinctive and non-distinctive components of the minority culture. Forces which in one context or period undermine some part of a minority culture in other contexts or periods have a conservative or supportive effect. Forces bearing powerfully upon one cultural component may have little or no bearing on another. For this reason sweeping statements about the relative strength of type forces acting on a minority-culture-as-a-whole are, on present evidence, unwise. It is more revealing, as the following section will illustrate, to focus on forces and changes in more specific social-and-cultural areas.

(C) THE EFFECTS OF THESE FORCES ON PRESENT-DAY MINORITY CULTURES

In small, simple, undifferentiated, unstratified societies, that is in societies where there is little concentration of resources and power, little division of labour, and no (or few) separate and specialised organisations (economic, political, administrative, religious, educational, recreational, etc.) most culture is *domestic culture.* It is based on family and kinship groups, and it is maintained, transmitted, used and modified in that sphere.

Because family and kinship groups in this case are multifunctional the domestic culture includes most of what might be called economic culture, political culture, religious culture, recreational culture and so on. This domestic culture tends—so far as the bulk of the inhabitants of the same sex and age group are concerned—to be uniform across the society. Most people have the same pattern or combination of cultural components.

Furthermore, because there is often little territorial mobility, and little contact with other societies-and-cultures, this culture tends to be local and largely distinctive to the people concerned. Because there is little social stratification there is little or no class culture. Again because of little stimulus it may be a static or slow moving culture.

It is surely clear that most of the cultural minorities of our time no longer live in societies of this kind nor do they possess cultures of the all-embracing domestic (or family and kinship) type.

They live for the most part in large, complex, differentiated, stratified societies, that is in societies where there has been considerable concentration of resources and power, much division of labour and the emergence of many separate and specialised organisations which operate largely independently of families and kinship groups. The culture of this society is a *multi-group culture.* It is based on a wide range of different groups (of which domestic groups are only one type) and it is maintained, transmitted, used and modified in very different (and not always interconnected) spheres.

There is obviously still a domestic culture but because many family functions over the years have come to be performed by specialist organisations it is no longer all-inclusive. Economic cultures, political cultures, administrative cultures, religious cultures, recreational cultures, etc. are in these societies largely the procedures, technology and ways of thought maintained, transmitted and modified by organisations. These are in a sense separate *organisational cultures.*

The multi-group culture of a modern society tends—so far as

the bulk of the inhabitants are concerned—to be multi-form. People no longer have the same pattern or combination of cultural components. Many different patterns are possible and many are adopted.

Today, because there is often considerable territorial mobility, and much contact with other societies-and-cultures, the multi-group culture tends to have both a wider territorial distribution and a wider territorial origin—that is it often has national and sometimes international as well as regional and local components. Similarly, because of social stratification, it may have different class components. For the same reasons the culture of any interrelated set of people in a modern society is very rarely completely or even predominantly distinctive to that set. Some of it, and sometimes much of it, is shared by other sets of people. Subject as it is to diverse and powerful forces of groups and organisations within and sometimes outside the society the culture is dynamic.

We have said enough, in previous sections, about the distinctive and, in most cases, even larger non-distinctive components of a minority culture. It remains to identify the social or group basis of particular cultural components and then to consider the effect on that group's culture of some of the internal and external social or group forces previously described.

We confine attention to the effect of governmental, political, economic, educational, religious, mass communication, recreational and domestic (family and kinship) forces on one *distinctive* component, *viz.* the minority's *mother language* and on one *non-distinctive* component, *viz.* the minority's *economic culture.* Hopefully, the same approach could be productively applied to the effects of these forces on any other component.

Having identified the group basis of a cultural component our approach was to explore the *influence* on the component of the forces of the more powerful groups. Indicators of group influence were taken to include: size of audience 'reached' by type force, exposure time (length, frequency and continuity of contact), positive reaction or active acceptance by people contacted (attendance, membership, patronage, purchase, adoption of belief or practice, use of channel and payment or other form of support), and negative reaction or active opposition (demonstrations, civil disobedience, strikes, boycotts and other forms of organised opposition to the force).

When this approach to the impact of forces on a distinctive

component of a minority culture is applied to the mother language of the minorities selected what does one find?

Two points are important to note here. First, language, unlike many other cultural components, is employed or may be employed in a range of different situations, e.g. domestic, recreational, educational, work, religious, political and so on. The influence of forces on its use or non-use needs to be examined in each situation in turn. Secondly, as earlier indicated, the forces operating on language-use in a particular situation should not be visualised as purely external or remote or centralised. They often include forces both external and internal to the minority, they may include close domestic groups, and may emanate not from a single, centralised source but from many regional or local centres like business firms, whether in majority or minority hands, which using the same modern methods (in this case business methods or economic culture) exert the same type of influence.

With regard to the minorities selected it was found that the operating forces *in toto* contributed to the conservation of the mother language, in most cases, in domestic, primary educational, religious, traditional literary and artistic production, and locally based economic situations; but that elsewhere, *viz.* in secondary and tertiary educational, national literary or artistic production, press, radio, television, cinema and gramophone recording, extra-locally-based economic, and political, governmental, legal and administrative situations the forces *in toto* contributed, in most cases and for the most part, to the use of other languages, most of them 'languages of wider communication'.

The more influential forces contributing to mother tongue preservation in the first set of situations seemed to be—*in the domestic situation*: families including those of kin, friends and neighbours; *in the primary educational situation*: families, and educational authorities, and sometimes language societies and other pressure or political groups; *in the religious situation*: families and religious organisations *in the traditional literary and artistic situation*: families, language and cultural societies and educational authorities; *and in the locally based economic situation*: minority-run economic organisations whether based on the family or not.

In all these situations most of the people involved used their mother tongue because they wanted to, because it appeared to be the most appropriate and useful to use under the circumstances, and because it was still possible to use it, one's companions on these occasions being largely of the same language group, and the authorities either supporting its use or not putting insurmountable obstacles in its way. In most of these cases there were no forces deliberately opposing the use of the minority language in these spheres.

It was obvious, however, in many cases, that mass media forces with their newspapers, comics, magazines, gramophone records and radio and television programmes employing other languages had already penetrated the home. There was evidence also, e.g. in Wales, that out-marriages sometimes introduced an important complicating factor. The evidence, however, was generally insufficient to support generalisations about any significant 'corrosive' or displacement trend due to these factors.

In the second set of situations the most influential forces contributing to the use of *other languages* seemed to be—in the *secondary and tertiary educational situation*: the educational authorities, and minority members themselves who prefer to adopt the other language in that context as a 'language of specialised information'; and in the other situations, *viz. national literary and artistic production, mass media, extra-local-economic, and political and governmental*: the controlling organisations, whether in private or public hands, and once again the minority members involved.

In all these situations *most* minority members (except among minorities like the French Canadians, South Tyrolese, Turkish Cypriots and the Afrikaners) use a language other than their own because they find it—in the wider multicultural situations concerned—the most appropriate and useful, and because government and the other controlling organisations, who cater for populations wider than the minority, understandably use and insist upon a language of wider communication.

What of the forces in the case of the exceptions mentioned which contributed to minority use of the *minority* language in these situations? The more influential seemed to be first, the minority people themselves who, possessing a language of 'wide utility' (French, German, Turkish, Afrikaans), a language of already proven value in higher education, art and literature, in the mass media, in business and in government, if not in the nation at least in a kin-state, wished to use it; secondly, a range of organisations in these fields, whether in the nation or the kin-state, who catering for a sufficiently large population, found it desirable and possible to use the language; and thirdly, the government which either encouraged or permitted its use.

Turning now from the effect of forces on a distinctive component, *viz.* the minority's mother language, we can more briefly consider the effect of forces on a non-distinctive component, *viz.* the minority's *economic culture.* As economic culture is a broad concept covering economic organisation, i.e. economic groups and their standardised activities and procedures; economic technology, i.e. plant, tools, machines, instruments and sources of power; and economic ideology, i.e. economic science and economic values e.g. with regard to the ownership of property or the control of the economy, it is desirable, and probably sufficient for our purposes, to concentrate on one part of it. We have chosen the *economic culture of a modern factory.*

With regard to this component, which was taken to be the more technical, operating system in factories of similar type, the most influential forces contributing to a 'non-distinctive' or broadly uniform factory culture seemed to be the owners (whether of the minority group or not) who often used generally similar modern methods, the supplying organisations and their advertising agents, technical-training institutions, and to a lesser extent government inspectorates, employers' organisations and trade unions who sometimes exerted a nationwide influence. In this area of culture as in many others in the non-distinctive sector a trend towards broad cultural convergence was clearly evident. Traditional minority culture in this national and sometimes international context seemed largely irrelevant. The cultural trend, here the technical trend, was a modernising one to which minority members like everyone else who was directly concerned generally subscribed.

(D) FEASIBLE MEASURES TO PROTECT MINORITY CULTURES

In the foregoing pages we have pointed out that there are very great differences between the structure and levels of development of minorities in relation to other cultural collectivities in their nation-states. This makes it very difficult to postulate a universally applicable theory of the future of minorities, and to suggest universally applicable measures for the preservation of their cultures.

We have also made it clear that apart from the extreme cases of physical or cultural genocide, the greatest problem facing cultural minorities is adaptation of their culture to an ever-increasing rate of economic, social and technological change, since if adaptation does not take place, the distinctive features of their separate identity—particularly language—may be eroded.

But before going on to outline what measures would be feasible, and in what circumstances, one preliminary point needs to be examined, namely, the justification for intervention. As has been indicated, the desire and determination of minorities to retain those elements of their distinctive culture which they believe to be valuable should certainly be a primary consideration. It is not the only one, however, nor need it be an essential one, for even if there is apathy and weakness of commitment among most members of a minority, there should surely be a wider concern, on the part of society at large, to preserve the culture in some form. It can surely be argued that the best justification for intervention on behalf of minority cultures is that they all in differing degrees are valuable and can contribute to the cultural enrichment of mankind.

Granted that this wider value is recognised, and that furthermore there is a desire and determination among members of minorities to preserve some components of their distinctive culture, certain measures applicable to all minorities, and other measures applicable to some minorities seem worth considering. In suggesting that these measures are feasible, the editors are claiming at least that demographic, economic, linguistic, psychological and political factors have been taken into account, and that therefore the measures are desired by the minority, are technically possible, and are politically permissible.

Language

Language is a key factor in the culture of almost all minorities, although many minority languages are of limited modern utility, as their speakers are the first to recognise, and this may affect their language commitment. However, either a hard core of dedicated speakers will usually exist, or the language will continue to be vigorously maintained in a number of private and public situations, such as those outlined in section (C) above. Therefore measures for language protection must have a high priority.

To begin with, it would be feasible to declare the language of the minority a *national* language. This would give status to the language, psychological reassurance to its users as to their place in the state, and enable it to receive support from the central government in various ways described below. The extent to which the language may be used as, or even declared an *official* language will clearly depend on the size of the minority and its degree of concentration, and these questions will also be examined below.[1]

If a language has a national status, and even more, if it has official status, then a framework is provided for it to thrive in written form and for its literature to develop, although there is, of course, no guarantee of this. What is important is to undertake anything that may halt the decay of a language as it is written, for it then becomes a marginal means of communication. It may survive as a spoken language, but under these circumstances the danger is that it will undergo a degenerative process *vis-à-vis* the dominant national language. Grammar and syntax may decline; geographical and social variants of words may come into being. Furthermore, without a national status to their language, the educated elites, the upper and middle classes, and the populations of towns, where higher levels of education are available, may well be induced to abandon it, so that it will continue to be spoken, if at all, by those living in the countryside or in outlying, dispersed areas—precisely those who would be least expected to write it or develop its literature.[2]

An important institutional means of seeing that the language is transmitted from one generation to another is the school. Children of the minority group, therefore, should at least be taught *in* their own language where this is desired and is practicable. The level at which such arrangements can be implemented will be linked to the modern utility of that language. Obviously it would be difficult to organise if the minority's families were scattered throughout the state, although in this case the Polish precedent between the wars may be cited, according to which schools or classes with teaching in the language would be established in the state system at primary level in any municipality if the parents of 40 children requested it, and at secondary level if the parents of 150 children requested it. The central government should ensure the availability of textbooks in the appropriate language, and see that they are kept up-to-date.

Where the minority is not only large in size, but is culturally cohesive to the extent of being overwhelmingly dedicated to the survival of its culture, and in addition, dominates numerically a definable geographical region, the minority language could be granted official status within the confines of that region.

Several important consequences would stem from such a situation. First, the region would become officially bilingual, or in exceptional cases, multilingual, and the public administration would have to provide services in these languages. Not only would this lead to greater understanding and efficiency in relations between the individual member of the minority and the administration, but the minority as a whole would receive a psychological uplift at evidence that the culture was still dominant in its own region and that respect for it was officially acknowledged as forming part of the national heritage. Any community which is governed through the medium of a language not its own has usually felt itself to some extent disenfranchised, and this feeling has always been a source of political agitation.[3]

Second, if language makes possible social organisation, and social organisation covers both private and professional activities, then a member of a minority would have the right also to use his own language at a place of work in his or her own homeland. Difficulties faced by a bilingual person who must work in his or her second language, according to the report of the Canadian Royal Commission on Bilingualism and Biculturalism, 'may be dramatic in their intensity—his sense of being diminished, the irritation that frequently results, and his loss of efficiency'.[4]

Third, at the administrative level it would be possible to introduce the principle of ethnic proportions for employment in public offices in the region, and to apply it both to regional government and to national institutions having a branch in the region. Service in the region should be safeguarded, if specifically requested, except in a few obvious cases such as careers in the armed forces and diplomatic corps.

Fourth, a framework would be created for a genuine bilingual and bicultural education system, in which all children in the region would learn both the national and the minority language from staff whose mother tongues were those languages. Furthermore, the minority language should count as a subject in its own right for university entrance requirements.

The administration of education

The editors were aware of the strong desire of most governments to control the education system, at least so as to ensure certain minimum standards and see that curricula respond to national requirements. They were also aware of the fear of governments that autonomous minority schools might be used as sources of anti-national feeling. It was felt that minorities should be represented on the basis of ethnic proportions on national and local education authorities and on school boards, with the right of obligatory consultation on the establishment and closing of schools and classes, the training and appointment of staff, choice of textbooks, and the way a subject should be taught, especially history.[5]

Minorities should also have the right to establish and control their own schools.

This raises the very delicate question of whether education should be segregated. It is to be noted that this is overwhelmingly the existing practice throughout the world, and efforts to end it have been strenuously resisted. The advocates of desegregation have argued that the lack of contact among children of the different groups leads to a mutual lack of knowledge and understanding that not only fuels the fires of any inter-group conflict but ensures that that conflict continues from generation to generation. Defenders of the system fear that desegregation might lead to weakening of respective cultural characteristics and group loyalties. The editors felt that since minorities were in the weaker situation as regards the maintenance and continuation of their culture, the choice should be theirs.

Mass media

With regard to the media, there should be provision for separate press, radio, and TV broadcasts.

In the case of the press, the minority should have at least one newspaper in its own language, with control of editorial policy, and facilities for publishing books. Factors such as frequency of issue of newspapers, type and numbers of books, and the extent of government subsidies (if any) would obviously depend on the size of the group, its relative degree of concentration, and its financial strength.

However, in a world where the spoken and audiovisual media are far superior sources of information than the written word, the need for minority languages to obtain an adequate place is even more vital. The problem is, of course, to decide what is 'adequate', and what is actually feasible to provide. For example, in multicultural states like Canada, Belgium and Switzerland (with the exception of the German minority in Belgium), each of the different cultures has an entire radio and television programme at its disposal, and it is noteworthy that the Italian-speaking population of Switzerland numbers less than three-quarters of a million, and only one-third lives in the Italian canton of Ticino. On the other hand, few minorities in western Europe enjoy really favourable radio and television services in their own language.[6]

The editors felt that minorities should have their own radio channel, and, where concentrated, at least a daily news bulletin and a weekly feature on TV, with control of the editorial policy concerned.

The arts

To the extent that the minority does not command the necessary resources, governmental support should be forthcoming for promotion of the minority's creative and performing arts. Here the editors had in mind the provision of support, first, for composers, playwrights, painters, craftsmen, etc.; secondly, for music, dance and drama performance; and thirdly, for the restoration and preservation of monuments, and objects of literary, artistic, and historical interest in libraries, galleries and museums. The importance of encouraging the arts through schools and festivals could not be overestimated. Responsibility for administration and policy should rest with the minority.

Population movement

Reference has already been made to the effect on indigenous culture when areas in which it is concentrated are invaded by bearers of another or the dominant culture.

In defence, minorities, especially those inhabiting areas with devolved government, have advocated that the regional authorities be able to control the issue of residence and work permits, restrict the purchase of land by outsiders, and have a veto over economic development projects. Other suggestions, not only by individuals but also by government, have aimed at creating as wide a degree of separation as possible, with the introduction of measures to ensure separate professional, institutional and sporting associations, the forbidding of mixed marriages, occupational segregation, and the gradual elimination of persons of other cultures from areas inhabited by the indigenous cultural group.

The editors appreciated that to almost all minorities 'outsiders' were often viewed as foreigners, and that it was the fear of the effects of economic and social development that made many minorities see a 'national park' solution as the only answer. They were also aware that some of the measures referred to above already exist in various parts of the world.

Nevertheless, the editors rejected such measures. They were aware that in general national governments were not in favour of sub-national authorities restricting the movement of citizens, except for reasons of health or public order. They felt that measures of social segregation could be practised voluntarily by the individual members of the minority if they so wished, but it would be a violation of human freedom to promote social segregation by law. Similarly, limitation of the right of the individual to dispose of his property to whom he pleased would be a very drastic measure, but if individual members of a minority felt sufficiently strongly about it they would not sell their land to outsiders and a *de facto* control would exist. As for occupational segregation, along the lines of South African *apartheid*, and the establishment of 'national parks' for various cultural groups, the problems created were likely to be just as great as those avoided—as the South African experience has shown. Finally, immigration was generally unlikely to occur in areas of poverty or high unemployment.

However, danger would exist when new large-scale development was planned for areas where the minority was concentrated, perhaps to expand existing sectors or to exploit newly discovered raw materials. Once again, the editors felt that it would be unrealistic to expect national governments to refrain from or temper such development. On the other hand, they should recognise the fear that many minorities have of being swamped or left behind during periods of economic and social transition, and certain steps should be taken to give the minority confidence in its future when these circumstances occur.

These steps might in some cases include the obligation to give priority to local inhabitants where applicants have equivalent qualifications for particular jobs.

The effect of industrial development projects on the social and cultural balance of the region should be taken into account. The editors were aware that central control and development of local natural resources has often been a source of grievance. But once again they felt that it was unrealistic to expect national governments to surrender control of such resources and their development to sub-national authorities or groups. Nevertheless, they felt that minorities must be consulted on regional economic development planning, especially in the case of investment by multinational companies.

In addition, technical and vocational education relevant to local needs should be developed to ensure that the human resource potential of the minority is adapted to meet the demands of the local economy. In this way the need for immigration of members of other cultures and emigration of members of the indigenous culture would be checked as far as possible.

Political measures

Cultural minorities have had to make many sacrifices in the past. In order to solve political problems they have been transferred against their will to the sovereignty of states of another culture. On grounds that they offend national unity, or are potential traitors, or have an allegedly lower—or even a higher—cultural level than that of the dominant or other groups in the state, they have been subjected to hostility, contempt, discrimination, and in some cases physical or cultural genocide. Their land and its resources have been exploited for ends with which they may not sympathise, and in ways which have left them the victims rather than the beneficiaries. They have almost always been subject to cultural, administrative, economic, social and political limitation—and sometimes humiliation—which they would not suffer if they were independent or belonged to a kin-state.

It is unsurprising, therefore, that minorities seek to limit as much as possible the effects of decisions by the national government, and to control their own destiny. Some see the only answer in secession from the state of which they are nationals, in order either to return to kin-states or to become independent. Others, taking into account national and international political and economic realities, and aware of existing precedents, have sought the answer in varying degrees of devolved government.

The editors felt that for cultures to live together in harmony, not only mutual understanding of the problems faced by the groups concerned but a resolution of mutual fears was essential. National governments would have to be convinced that any measures adopted would not fatally undermine their authority and lead to a break up of their state. Minorities would be seeking, on the other hand, positive action, including measures of reverse discrimination if necessary, to enable them to repair the damages of past ill treatment, exploitation and discrimination, and to retrieve lost ground if at an economic and social disadvantage *vis-à-vis* the dominant or other cultures.

What constitutional arrangement would best enable policies of reverse discrimination, the protection of group cultural, economic and social interests, and the matching of law with local cultural norms to be implemented?

The editors were convinced that the way to a satisfactory solution lay in granting areas with cultural minorities, whether within a federal or unitary framework, as high a degree of devolved government as possible. If governments have the legitimate right to demand loyalty from their citizens of the minority, they have the corresponding and necessary duty of responding to the legitimate demands of the minority, however weak or strong that minority may be, so that dissatisfaction does not rise so high that the minority comes to feel it can only obtain a response by threatening to withdraw that loyalty.[7]

Devolved government would provide a politically identifiable framework within which it would be easier for the minority to ensure that the distinctive features of its culture that are valuable and viable are preserved and developed, and to ensure that it can assume greater responsibility for its own future.

NOTES

1. The constitutions of Switzerland (Art. 116) and Ireland (Art. 8) distinguish between national and official languages. The basic difference is that whereas official languages are used in administrative relations throughout the state, use of national languages may be restricted territorially or institutionally. In the case of Switzerland Romansh was declared a national language in 1938, 'in order to provide legal federal support for its protection'.
   P. Bernard, *Etude Comparative sur la protection des minorités* (Lyons, 1976), pp. 110–14.

2. cf. R. Petrella, *The Regions of Europe*, EEC Document X/467/76F/(Brussels, 1976), p. 94.
3. *Report of the Canadian Royal Commission on Bilingualism and Biculturalism* (Ottawa, 1967), pp. xxix.
4. *Ibid.*, pp. xxix-xx.
5. Dispossessing minority groups of their history is a well known device for ensuring cultural uniformity and destroying cultural diversity. One of the faults of modern times is to teach that our nations have existed since time immemorial, and that the march of history, after some dark ages, is a natural process leading to the growth of nations and their definitive consolidation into sovereign states delimited by natural frontiers. Thus in French schools one learns not about France and the people who live there but about the French state, from the Capets to the fifth Republic, from the point of view of its unity. Petrella, *op. cit.*, pp. 22–24.
6. As regards radio, the South Tyrolese (145 hours per week), the Catalans (46 hours per week diffused by two stations), the Spanish Basques (27½ hours per week diffused by four stations), and the Welsh (17 hours per week) are the best off. Most other minorities – the French Basques, Bretons, Corsicans, Scots Gaelic, Frisians, Friulans, Occitans, Sards, and the French-speaking Italians of Val d'Aosta – receive less than 4 hours per week. In the case of television the South Tyrolese (14 hours per week) and the Welsh (13 hours per week) are again the best off. The other minorities receive transmissions of anything from three hours every two weeks to no television time at all. Petrella, *op. cit.*, pp. 160 ff.

   Minorities with cultural kin-states nearby are, of course, in a much stronger position than those with none. The South Tyrolese can pick up radio and TV programmes from Switzerland, Austria and West Germany, while the inhabitants of Val d'Aosta can obtain French-speaking programmes from France and the *Suisse Romande*. The case for providing radio and TV services in the language of the minority will therefore be all the more important in the case of minorities with no cultural kin-state. However, another perhaps not irrelevant point may be made. A kin-state will certainly provide cultural support for its brethren in another state, but not necessarily continual news and features unless a crisis situation exists. Yet provision of news and features about themselves in their own language from their own sources will give minorities a sense of psychological security. To deny facilities to a minority on the grounds that radio and TV programmes can be picked up from the kin-state will only create a gulf between the minority and the central government, or widen an existing one, by encouraging the minority to look to the other side of the border for its sources of information and its picture of the world.
7. A. E. Alcock, Protection of Minorities: Three Case Studies (Northern Ireland Constitutional Convention, Belfast, 1975).

Select Bibliography

A. E. Alcock, *The History of the South Tyrol Question* (London, 1970).

A. E. Alcock, 'A New Look at Protection of Minorities and the Principle of Equality of Human Rights', *Community Development Journal*, vol. 12, no. 2 (April 1977), pp. 85–95.

A. E. Alcock, *Protection of Minorities: Three Case Studies* (Northern Ireland Constitutional Convention, Belfast 1975).

C. W. Anderson, F. R. von der Mehden and C. Young, *Issues of Political Development* (Englewood Cliffs, 1964).

C. Bagley, *The Dutch Plural Society* (London, 1973).

T. H. Bagley, *General Principles and Problems in the International Protection of Minorities* (Geneva, 1950).

B. Berelson and G. A. Steiner, *Human Behaviour, an Inventory of Scientific Findings* (New York, 1964).

I. D. Duchacek, *Comparative Federalism, The Territorial Dimension of Politics* (New York, 1970).

I. D. Duchacek, *Rights and Liberties in the World Today* (Santa Barbara, 1973).

R. Emerson, *From Empire to Nation* (Boston, 1960).

M. J. Esman, *Administration and Development in Malaysia: Institution Building and Reform in a Plural Society* (Syracuse, 1972).

W. M. Evan (ed.), *Law and Sociology* (New York, 1962).

J. A. Fishman (ed.), *Advances in Language Planning* (The Hague, 1974).

C. Geertz, *Old Societies and New States* (New York, 1963).

M. M. Gordon, *Assimilation in American Life* (New York, 1964).

A. L. Kroeber and C. Kluckhorn, 'Culture, a critical review of concepts and definitions', *Ethnology*, vol. 47, no. 1 (1952).

B. Malinowski, *A Scientific Theory of Culture* (Chapel Hill, 1944).

P. Mayo, *The Roots of Identity* (London, 1974).

Minority Rights Group, Series of Reports (London, 1971–77).

E. S. Munger, *Afrikaner and African Nationalism* (London, 1967).

E. A. Nordlinger, *Politics and Society, Studies in Comparative Political Sociology* (Englewood Cliffs, 1970).

A. W. Orridge, *Peripheral Nationalism* (Berlin, 1977).

C. Palley, 'Constitutional Devices in Multi-racial and Multi-religious Societies', *Northern Ireland Legal Quarterly*, vol. 19 (1968), pp. 377–417.

C. Palley, 'Law and the Unequal Society', *Race,* vol. 21 (1971), pp. 16–47, 139–67.

R. Petrella, *The Regions of Europe*, EEC Document X/467/76F/ (Brussels, 1976).

G. Price, *The Present Position of Minority Languages in Western Europe: A Select Bibliography* (Cardiff, 1969).

Report of the Canadian Royal Commission on Bilingualism and Biculturalism (Ottawa, 1967).

R. A. Schermerhorn, *Comparative Ethnic Relations* (New York, 1965).

G. E. Simpson and J. M. Yinger, *Racial and Cultural Minorities* (New York, 1965).

M. G. Smith, *The Plural Society in the British West Indies* (Berkeley, 1965).

M. Stephens, *Linguistic Minorities in Western Europe* (Llandysul, 1976).

M. Straka (ed.), *Handbuch der Europäischen Volksgruppen* (Vienna, 1970).

J. Tunstall (ed.), *Media Sociology* (London, 1970).

E. Tylor, Sir, *Primitive Culture* (London, 1871).

C. Wagley and M. Harris, *Minorities in the New World* (New York, 1958).

R. L. Watts, *New Federations. Experiments in the Commonwealth* (Oxford, 1966).

W. H. Whiteley (ed.), *Problems of Multilingualism with special reference to Eastern Africa* (Oxford, 1971).

L. Wirth, 'The Problem of Minority Groups', in R. Linton (ed.), *The Science of Man in the World Crisis* (New York, 1945).

Index of Proper Names

Index of Subjects